Fivefold
Ministry
made practical

How to release apostles, prophets, evangelists,
pastors and teachers to equip today's church

Ron Myer

House to House Publications
www.h2hp.com

Fivefold Ministry Made Practical

by Ron Myer

© 2006, 2017 by DOVE Itnernational

Published by
House to House Publications
11 Toll Gate Road, Lititz, PA, 17543 USA
Toll-free: 800-848-5892
www.h2hp.com

ISBN 10: 1-886973-57-1
ISBN 13: 978-1-886973-57-2

Printed in the United States of America

Dedication

This book is dedicated to
all the faithful fivefold ministers
within DOVE International.
Your wholeheartedness and commitment to seeing the church
conformed to the image of God are encouraging and inspiring.

Acknowledgments

Thank you, my Lord Jesus Christ who has given me life and life abundantly and protects me in all of my travels.

To my parents, Hershey and Anna Mary, who have prayed for me every day of my life and have trained me in my early years to walk in the ways of the Lord.

A big "thank you" to the love of my life, Bonnie, who has stayed home on many occasions with our six children allowing me the freedom to travel and minister.

To our children—Kevin and Lisa Hurst, Keith and Teaa, Daryl and Tabitha, Mark and Lindsay, Duane and Brian—you guys are an inspiration to me!

To Larry Kreider, my spiritual father and friend, who encouraged me to write this book in the first place and continued to inspire me throughout the process.

A special thanks goes to Karen Ruiz, editor, and Sarah Sauder for cover design and layout, without whom this book would not be a reality.

To my personal intercessors who prayed me through as the book unfolded.

Thank you to many others who gave valuable insights to the book, including: Tom Barnett, Peter Bunton, Shirley Hampton, Karen Hugo, Monte Jones, Larry Kreider, Gil Miller, Steve Prokopchak, Dave Redish, Brian Sauder and Keith Yoder.

Last but not least, thanks to the proofreaders: Denise Sensenig, Carolyn Sprague and Tracy Stoltzfus.

Contents

Foreword

I know of no other book published on the fivefold ministry that is so biblical and practical for the church of our generation. This is not a book about theory. It is the real deal.

Ron Myer has a broad range of leadership experience. He has served as a senior pastor of a local church and ministered trans-locally both nationally and internationally as a modern day prophet and apostle. He has tasted the grass from both sides of the fence, and he has lived to tell the story!

I have been honored to serve alongside Ron in Christian leadership for the past twenty years. He practices what he preaches. Whether he is solving problems, riding his motorcycle, preaching, mentoring leaders or prophesying, he does so with great wisdom, faith, and enthusiasm, along with a heart of compassion and grace. Ron is leading the way for many in the arena of fivefold ministry as the Lord restores and releases His healthy apostles, prophets, evangelists, pastors and teachers among us. We desperately need the equipping ministry of these five God-given gifts. The church will not come into unity and maturity without them. The Lord is opening the hearts of local church pastors and elders to utilize the ministry of these specialized ministers who have paid the price to be equipped, molded by the Spirit and properly connected to His church.

As you read, be sure to use a highlighter pen. You will go back to the truths that jump off the pages again and again.

—Larry Kreider, International Director
DOVE International

Introduction

When Jesus left this earth, He left the church with a job to do—spread the gospel to the whole earth. He didn't leave church with only a vision and purpose. He gave her the tools to get the job done. Jesus specifically gave the church, among other things, the gifts of apostle, prophet, evangelist, pastor and teacher.

In this book, I share a vision for the fivefold ministry and how it was created to function within the local church. Depending on your spiritual background or theological understanding, the term "fivefold ministry" may not mean anything to you. Or, you may be very familiar with the term and hope to gain further insight on the development of your personal gift of apostle, prophet, evangelist, pastor or teacher. Perhaps as a church leader you are seeking to develop the fivefold ministry for your church. Whether this term is new or familiar, I believe *Fivefold Ministry Made Practical* will help you to sort through what the fivefold ministry is and what it is not.

My goal is to help those who are involved in fivefold ministry to be even more effective than they currently are and have a greater understanding of the gift that is stirring within them. This book also will help those who have never heard of the fivefold ministry to expand their horizons so they can catch a glimpse of these precious gifts that Jesus Christ has given to the church for the advancement of His kingdom.

Kingdom work is fun! I am the kind of person who throws himself wholeheartedly into what I believe is my life's work. I believe God wants us to be enthusiastic about the gifts He has given us. We should love what we are doing. I love what I do, and I hope that my enthusiasm about fivefold ministry comes through in the pages ahead.

It was not always that way. I did not understand that God gave me gifts that He expected me to use. Although I grew up in a solid Christian home, I realized shortly after I got married that my wife, Bonnie, was much more passionate about Jesus and the kingdom of God than I was. I knew I needed some adjustments in my life. Then in 1982, God sovereignly poured His Spirit on me, and I had a fervent encounter with Jesus.

At the time, I was part of a partnership that owned and operated a large dairy farm in Pennsylvania, and increasingly the Lord began to give me opportunities to minister to people. Although I had accepted Jesus into my life at 12 years of age and been actively involved in a local church, I never heard any mention of the fivefold ministry gifts other than *pastor* and *evangelist*.

Consequently, when I became aware of the ministry gifts developing in my life, I knew little about them. Still, the Lord continued to allow me to minister to people, and the fivefold gifts continued to develop. I have experienced the most exciting times over the past two decades as I developed into an apostolic prophetic fivefold minister. I have clearly observed the Lord restoring the fivefold ministry to the church today.

The form and function of fivefold ministry is often misunderstood in the modern day church, and there have been false starts and mistakes made by both fivefold ministers and other leaders relating to them. Nevertheless, the Lord is helping us to learn from our mistakes. He is giving us wisdom to empower these ministers and ministries so they may work with the local church as the Lord intended. With the increasing emphasis on the fivefold ministry, the Lord is doing a tremendous work in releasing these ministers into the body of Christ.

We are learning, but there is so much more to learn. While we have a long way to go, there *are* a lot of things we *have* learned. That's why I wrote this book. I also want to share with you some of the problems we have encountered, disappointments, difficulties, misunderstandings, failures and how we adapted along the way. In all of it, we have kept pressing on knowing that Jesus has given these gifts to His body, and we are willing to persevere to see them released and functioning properly.

It is my desire that spiritual leaders would read this book and gain a greater understanding and ability to release the fivefold ministry in their midst in their own local churches.

Let's learn how proven fivefold ministers function, along with practical ways church leadership can relate to them as they minister in our churches and small groups. It's time to take what we have learned and put it into practice!

To make the text easier to read, I use the masculine gender when speaking of fivefold ministers or other leaders in the church. For the record, I believe fivefold ministry is not gender-specific, and women can serve in the fivefold ministry. Some examples in the Bible are Junia in Romans 16:7 and Priscilla in Acts 18:26.

—Ron Myer, International Apostolic Council
DOVE International
11 Toll Gate Road
Lititz, PA 17543

CHAPTER 1

Jesus Gives Gifts
to the Church

Do you like taking risks? I do. When I was a kid, I jumped my bicycle over everything I could find. As a teenager, whatever I drove—tractor, car, truck or bike—I drove as fast as I could. Before I had a driver's license, I would drive the car out our farm's long dirt lane to get the mail. It was not uncommon for me to hit 55 mph before the first speed bump, but I wanted to go faster! I begged my parents to buy me a motorcycle so I could really have fun. They wouldn't allow it. They were afraid, and rightfully so, that I would hurt myself.

Shortly after I got married, I bought my first motorcycle. This was the life for me! Motorcycles satisfied my need for speed. Riding up and down steep steps and climbing high hills through trees and rocks was thrilling. Shifting through the gears with a powerful piece of steel screaming underneath me got my adrenaline going. Over the years, I had a lot of fun on motorcycles, and there were times that I took risks. Sometimes the risks were exhilarating with an appreciable amount of air between my bike and the ground. Other times the risks were not as fun. There was blood and pain, bones to mend, and metal to be fixed. Not every risk paid off.

As with the motorcycle, I have taken other risks in my life as well. Some of them paid off, and some didn't work out too well.

I have discovered that I need to take risks in order to extend the kingdom of God. I believe one of the key ingredients to thrusting the kingdom of God forward is for people to be willing to become risk-takers. Businesses are started because someone is willing to take a risk. In the same way, churches are planted because someone is willing to step out boldly and try something that is out-of-the-ordinary. I took a tremendous risk when I gave up my life's dream of farming in order to fulfill my life's call today.

I believe the Lord wants you to be a risk-taker because He is a risk-taker. He takes a risk every time He blesses us. When He took the children of Israel into the promised land, He reminded them that when they were full of blessings, they should not forget Who brought them there. When Jesus blesses us, He takes a risk that we become secure in our blessings and forget the very One who gave them to us.

When Jesus ascended from the earth 2,000 years ago, He took an enormous risk. He delegated the responsibility for spreading the good news of the gospel to a few disciples. Why did He entrust the very expansion of the kingdom of God into the hands of a small number of young and immature men? How did He know they could do it? What if they messed up? They had made so many mistakes while He was here. How would they ever function without His guidance? They had trouble enough in understanding the Word of God, much less teaching it so that others could comprehend it.

The truth is that Jesus gave very clear instructions for the disciples before He actually passed His mantle on to them. Although He left them with a job to do—spread the gospel throughout the world—He didn't leave them unequipped for that task. He pledged to provide what they needed to accomplish it.

The missing piece was the Holy Spirit, and Jesus promised to send the Spirit to the young church. He very specifically told them not to leave the city of Jerusalem until they were "endued with power from on high."[1] Only after that could the young disciples carry out the expansion of the kingdom.

It was as Jesus promised—the Holy Spirit came powerfully at Pentecost and empowered the church with spiritual gifts to go and do all that Jesus had set forth for her to do. And the rest, as they say, is history! In fact, let's look back at the early church and the events that shaped history as Christians endeavored to accomplish the task of spreading the gospel to the whole world.

The cost of expanding the kingdom of God

Somewhere around 30 A.D. Jesus died on the cross. By 70 A.D., most of the known world had already heard the gospel of Jesus Christ preached to them in their language; however, this was not a safe time to become a Christian. The Roman Emperor, Nero, was dipping Christians in wax and using them for human torches in his garden.

> ... there began a carnival of blood such as even heathen Rome never saw before or since.... A 'vast multitude' of Christians was put to death in the most shocking manner. Some were crucified, some sewn up in animal skins and thrown to the dogs, some were covered in pitch, nailed to wooden posts, and burned as torches. It was in the fallout of this that Peter and Paul gave their lives for their Savior, probably within a year of each other.[2]

Being a follower of Christ meant that your life was at risk. Christians were being persecuted severely. It wasn't Monday night football; it was Monday night at the Coliseum with Christians versus the lions—and the lions were winning! People were laying down their lives for their faith in Jesus Christ.

The apostle Paul gives evidence to this dangerous time in his letter to the Hebrew Christians.

> ... you endured a great struggle with sufferings: partly while you were made a spectacle both by reproaches and tribulations, and partly while you became companions of those who were so treated; for you had compassion on me in my

chains, and joyfully accepted the plundering of your goods, knowing that you have a better and an enduring possession for yourselves in heaven.... (Hebrews 10:32-34 NKJV).

Paul acknowledges that when the early Christians received the revelation of Jesus Christ as Lord, their lives were opened up to great struggles and sufferings. He mentions that some of their afflictions occurred because of the very fact that they made Jesus Christ the Lord of their lives, and some of their sufferings came from associating with others who had already made that decision. Either way, the life of the early Christian was one of conflict and difficulty.

It cost Christ and the early church dearly to expand and extend the kingdom of God, and it should not surprise us that there is still a price we have to pay. I encounter many Christians today who mistakenly think that everything should be handed to them without a struggle. Their mindset tells them life should work out the way they want it. After all, they have the Holy Spirit; they have faith; they have the anointing from the Holy One. What is wrong with this line of reasoning?

The truth is that the early church had the anointing and was full of faith too. Even though they were full of the Holy Spirit, which empowered them to accomplish the things they were doing, everything did not always go as they had planned. They got thrown into prison and were beaten; however, God used the events that happened to work out His glory.

My wife, Bonnie, and I have been through many difficult times individually and as a family. Yet we have learned so much by going through those demanding times. God has always shown Himself strong in every situation. It wasn't always pleasant, it certainly wasn't easy, but we have always grown as we kept our eyes focused on Him, looking to the Lord to see us through the circumstances facing us.

Paul understood suffering because he experienced it firsthand. He was put in chains. Other early Christians, because of their relationship with Paul, joyfully accepted the plundering of their goods. Their earthly possessions were randomly confiscated by the government, all because of their faith in the Lord Jesus Christ. And Paul says they did it joyfully![3]

Many people today struggle with merely paying taxes to the government. They do everything they can to wiggle out of them or at least postpone them. Compare that with the early Christians who had all of their life's possessions confiscated. In great faith, they laid down their rights because they had received the expansive revelation of the love of the Lord Jesus Christ.

Miracles abound—the church matures

Despite widespread persecution, however, the church continued to grow and expand. The church proceeded to mature, churches were planted, people were saved, leadership was established and miracles continued to happen. In the midst of this difficult time, the church exploded in numbers and moved forward.

The early church was a vibrant church. It was a church brimming with excitement and anticipation. Everyone depended on each other. Their lives depended upon their relationships, and their life source was in small groups meeting together in homes. Their prayer life was passionate. They believed in the miraculous, because without the miraculous, they would not have survived.

Fellow Christians fervently prayed for one another when they had encounters with people hostile to Christianity. The church was growing, expanding, encountering darkness, and living the miraculous as they depended upon one another on an everyday basis.

What happened to the ministry of every believer?

Then something happened that changed the life of every Christian. The Roman emperor Constantine converted to Christianity. Under him, the Edict of Milan (313 A.D.) was sent forth to "... grant both the Christians and to all others full authority to follow whatever worship each man has desired." Suddenly, the tables were turned. It was no longer a hardship to be a Christian. In fact, it became fashionable. Everyone wanted to become a Christian because it seemed everyone else was one.

Constantine, in his zeal, marched his whole army through a river baptizing every one of them and declaring that they were now "Christian." The church was growing at such a rapid pace that Constantine built the first church building in 323 A.D. to handle the masses that were coming to Christ. Leaders were put in charge of the church gatherings, and eventually ministry was taken out of the hands of the people and placed in the hands of the elite few who could lead these larger gatherings.

If this sounds familiar, it is because it is the look of much of the church today. Too often, down through the church ages, ministry was relegated to a few and the remainder of the church took on a spectator mentality. For the last 1,700 years, I believe the Holy Spirit has been trying to place ministry back into the hands of common, ordinary people.

Paul says in Ephesians 4:12, that Jesus gave the apostle, prophet, evangelist, pastor and teacher, *"for the equipping of the saints for the work of ministry, for the edifying of the body of Christ"* (NKJV).

One of the major truths that Christians need to understand is that Jesus Christ wants to equip them for the work of ministry. Ministry should occur through every person's life. Our homes should be ministry centers. We need to see our workplaces as places that are full of ministry opportunities. Our relationships are key to the expanding of the kingdom of God. Jesus wants us to carry Him wherever we go and into all our relationships. He wants us to know and understand that where we are, the kingdom of God is. Additionally, where the kingdom of God is, His power is. Where His power is, He will bring about change!

Spiritual gifts empower us for service

Christ invites all Christians to minister both inside and outside the church and gives us spiritual gifts to do it. It is the Lord's plan for His people to be empowered for service in the church and in the world. His Word reveals a victorious church made up of believers working together, each doing his or her part in advancing the kingdom of God on this earth. God has designed the church so that we are dependent on each other, just as the early church was. We need each other and the various gifts that God gives so we can reach spiritual maturity.

A contemporary church that is relevant and reaches the needs of the community around it encourages every believer to be involved and use their gifts. D.L. Moody (1837-99) understood this truth years ago when he said, "I would rather put a hundred men to work than do the work of a hundred men!" He realized the importance of the ministry of all believers. As one man, he could only do so much work, but with the help of many others who understood that they were also ministers, he could multiply himself.

Jesus in effect said the same when He left earth. He said that it was expedient that He went because He would send the Holy Spirit to help us so that we could do His work on earth (John 14:16). As long as Jesus was here, it was just Him, full of the Holy Spirit, working. But when He left, He sent the Holy Spirit to fill many, many believers to be testimonies of Him.

In other words, He was multiplying those who could do the work of ministry here on the earth. When each member of the body of Christ faithfully exercises his or her spiritual gifts, each contributes to the church's overall health and growth.

CHAPTER 2

A Gift for Everyone

I recently noticed a cute teddy bear being offered at an airport stand as a free gift for signing up for a credit card. Why give away a gift? Research proves that people will open their wallets and buy when gift-with-purchase sales are offered because they feel as if they get something extra, for which they do not pay. The free gift makes them feel like a winner.

Everyone enjoys receiving a gift. A gift expresses different sentiments such as love, friendship or respect, and usually there is a specific purpose in giving one. Spiritual gifts given by God are much the same. They are an expression of love from God to us and have a specific purpose behind each gift.

God has blessed each person with spiritual gifts, but no one person can possess the fullness of all of them. That's why we should work together. We need everyone's gift so we can be fully equipped for service.

The gifts God gives are to be used as tools. They are given to every individual, and we will not fully see the kingdom of God advance until all members in the body use their gifts to do their God-appointed work. The church consists of many members working together, empowered by the gifts given to them to serve others.

Distinguishing among the gifts

But how do we distinguish among all the supernatural gifts we find in the Bible? What do we do with our gifts? Ask any gathering of Christians for a show of hands of those who know what their spiritual gifts are, and you will get a few hands raised and the rest stare at you blankly. We should all know what our spiritual gifts are. How can we use them if we do not know what they are? Understanding the kinds of gifts God gave to the church is important. Associated with each list of gifts is a comment on unity and diversity in the body of Christ which leads to maturity in the process.

A study of the Bible will reveal that God gives many different kinds of spiritual gifts. Some gifts are inner motivational gifts that God gives each individual. Others help believers to "do the work of ministry," and yet other special ministry gifts are given to individual leaders to "train God's people to do the work of the ministry." In brief, here are the three groups and their functions:

Gifts of the Father
Motivational: Inner motivational gifts God gives to individuals
Romans 12:3-8

Gifts of the Holy Spirit
Operational: Gifts to help believers do the work of ministry
1 Corinthians 12:7-11

Gifts of Christ
Fivefold: Gifts for individual leaders to train God's people to do the work of the ministry
Ephesians 4:9-16

Although the fivefold gifts of Christ are the focus of this book, let's first briefly explore the other kinds of gifts: the motivational gifts and the operational gifts.

Gifts of the Father—motivational gifts

It is commonly understood that every person has a motivational gift, or, as some say, a gift that carries a thumbprint of God the Father in his or her life. This very imprint of God is an affirmation that each individual has been created in His image.

This imprint is illustrated in the story of Mary and Martha; Martha was motivated by serving and Mary was motivated by mercy. Their differing motivations and tasks caused them to come into conflict, because Martha complained, "She sits at your feet while I do the dishes."

Our differing motivational gifts cause us to be energized in a certain direction or look at things from a particular perspective. We need to recognize our gifts because they are essential in ministering to others. We find the listing of these gifts in Romans 12:3-8 (NKJV):

> For I say, through the grace given to me, to everyone who is among you, not to think of himself more highly than he ought to think, but to think soberly, as God has dealt to each one a measure of faith. For as we have many members in one body, but all the members do not have the same function, so we, being many, are one body in Christ, and individually members of one another. Having then gifts differing according to the grace that is given to us, let us use them: if prophecy, let us prophesy in proportion to our faith; or ministry, let us use it in our ministering; he who teaches, in teaching; he who exhorts, in exhortation; he who gives, with liberality; he who leads, with diligence; he who shows mercy, with cheerfulness.

Paul says that the grace of God given to each individual is shown in different gifts. Each of these is a special talent for a particular type of activity. I believe this conveys that everyone on the face of the earth has one or more of these gifts. The Lord longs for each individual to use his or her God-given motivational gift for Him, even though not everyone does.

Since these gifts are not dependent on our relationship with Jesus but upon the fact that we have been created in God's image, they are given to believers and unbelievers alike. Think about it. There are countless fantastic teachers in this world who have a wonderful gift of teaching, but they may not yet be believers. Their gift, however, gives evidence that they have been created in God's image.

We have all heard of people who have given away millions of dollars. Although they give money to schools, universities, hospitals, local communities, libraries and many other worthy causes, they are not necessarily Christians. However, it does give evidence that they are created in God's image and are gifted in giving. They give millions of dollars away because the thumbprint of God on their lives prompts them to be generous givers.

Some time ago, there was a TV show where a successful businessman gave away a million dollars to an individual. Why would somebody do that? Granted, there can be countless ulterior motivations for giving away that kind of money on national television, but one reason is that this individual has an ability and desire to give. It comes from an inner motivation.

How about someone who ministers? There are many doctors and nurses and other social service employees who minister to people tirelessly. Some of them are very effective in their ministry, but they may not yet be Christians. They have a thumbprint on their lives to minister to others and are good at it.

We have all met people in our lives who are naturally optimistic and excellent encouragers. But not all of them have a personal relationship with Jesus—they just seem to have it in them to speak timely words of motivation that cheer and inspire us. In fact, it is regrettable, but sometimes Christians are less encouraging than non-Christians. Believers in Jesus should be the best encouragers of all. We should be continually inspiring others to be like Christ and fulfill their destiny in God.

What about the motivational gift of prophecy and prophesying? There are individuals, Christian and non-Christian alike, who have the ability to sense where things are heading; they seem to intuitively know that "if we do not change things in this town, we are going to have such and such a problem." This is a kind of prophecy or sensing of the times.

Secular journals are filled with writings that speak in a prophetic sense concerning the future of a nation, for example. They examine the current situation and get a sense of where a particular country is headed and make declarations and suggestions for change. Again, this speaks to and affirms that every person has been created in the image of God.

The Lord wants us to use these gifts for Him, and the fact that every individual has gifts gives evidence that they have been created in the image of our Father God. So we fittingly call these the "Father's gifts."

Gifts of the Holy Spirit—gifts of operations

The nine spiritual gifts found in 1 Corinthians 12:7-11 are not only nine gifts given for individual use but also gifts in which the Holy Spirit manifests Himself through people to enable them to help others. These gifts are sometimes called "gifts of operations."

> But the manifestation of the Spirit is given to each one for the profit of all: for to one is given the word of wisdom through the Spirit, to another the word of knowledge through the same Spirit, to another faith by the same Spirit, to another gifts of healings by the same Spirit, to another the working of miracles, to another prophecy, to another discerning of spirits, to another different kinds of tongues, to another the interpretation of tongues. But one and the same Spirit works all these things, distributing to each one individually as He wills (NKJV).

In these verses, the Bible mentions that the Holy Spirit disperses gifts so that they can be used to promote the health, healing and wholeness in the whole body. When you are saved, I believe you receive at least one of these nine spiritual gifts in your life. They are evidence that you have made Jesus the Lord of your life and the Holy Spirit has come and taken up residence.

The Spirit of God gives these gifts as He pleases so that the gifts may be used for the common good. In other words, they are not for our private advantage or exclusive profit, but they are used for the common benefit of others.

Many people are not aware of what their gifts are and consequently do not function in their gifts. This, however, does not mean that the gifts are not present. Often, because of ignorance, insecurity or seemingly inability to use their gifts, people fail to experience what God desires to do in and through them. Often, Christians pray the simple prayer, "Lord, use me," but they are unaware of their gifts (God's supernatural ability), and with opportunities all around, they sit idle, and the needs go unmet.

I love it when the Lord uses the gifts He has given me to be a blessing to others. God wants us to be aware that the gifts exist, that we possess them, and that the Holy Spirit will manifest Himself through us. When we ask the Holy Spirit to fill us, dwell in us and give us a new dimension of His power, the gifts are released in our lives in a greater way. Being filled with the Holy Spirit empowers us to use these gifts we may never have realized we had before!

These nine gifts are to be used for ministry to others. We position ourselves as vessels who give the Holy Spirit the freedom to move freely in us and through us. We can be the key to the Holy Spirit ministering in someone's life.

Each of these gifts is a manifestation of the Holy Spirit. Each requires a power that is not natural to man. It is a supernatural power that comes from God alone, namely the Holy Spirit. The word of wisdom, the word of knowledge, healings, workings of miracles—these are all gifts that only the Holy Spirit can accomplish. He desires to manifest Himself through every believer in order to give testimony of the resurrection power of Jesus. But we must allow Him to work through us to benefit others. There have been times where the Lord has given me a word of knowledge in a situation that alerts me to something about an individual that I had no natural way of knowing. Bringing this information to light and praying with the individual often was the key to his or her healing.

Let me share one more thought about these supernatural gifts. Many spiritual leaders have primarily encouraged believers to use these gifts in the church for the benefit of others within the body of Christ. However, these gifts were given not just for the benefit of the church but for every believer to also use in ministry to the unsaved.

A number of years ago, I was conducting a small group leaders' retreat with my friends in Ohio. As we broke for lunch, the pastor started going around the room asking people if they had a word for June (not her real name). "Who is June?" I asked.

"She is one of the waitresses serving us today," the pastor responded. "I believe God has a word for her today."

June was not a Christian, but she agreed to let us pray for her when we asked. We gathered around her and began to pray. Someone received a word of knowledge about something in her past. Within minutes, tears flowed down her cheeks as the Lord ministered to that past hurt in her life. Yes, the gifts can have an awesome impact on the unsaved, helping them to face spiritual reality.

The Gifts of Christ—fivefold gifts

This brings us to the fivefold gifts, the central subject of this book. These gifts that Jesus gave to the church are often referred to as the *fivefold ministry gifts* because there are five of them and they not only are representative of distinct people and ministerial functions, but they also reveal five principles for effective ministry. The apostle, prophet, evangelist, pastor and teacher represent the principles of governing, guiding, gathering, guarding and grounding.

> And He Himself gave some to be apostles, some prophets, some evangelists, and some pastors and teachers, for the equipping of the saints for the work of ministry, for the

edifying of the body of Christ, till we all come to the unity of the faith and of the knowledge of the Son of God, to a perfect man, to the measure of the stature of the fullness of Christ; that we should no longer be children, tossed to and fro and carried about with every wind of doctrine, by the trickery of men, in the cunning craftiness of deceitful plotting, but, speaking the truth in love, may grow up in all things into Him who is the head Christ. (Ephesians 4:11-16 NKJV).

In mentioning the gifts of Christ, we notice it says that He gave "some" to be apostles, prophets, evangelists, pastors and teachers. Not everyone will receive the gifts of leadership mentioned here. While *every* person on the face of the earth has at least one of the "Father's gifts," the thumbprint of being created in God's image, and *every* believer has a gift(s) of the Holy Spirit giving evidence to the fact of having the Holy Spirit in him, only *some* will develop the fivefold gifts.

Before we elevate them to an exclusive rank, we must grasp that the fivefold gifts are not *offices* but *functions* of ministry. Jack Hayford makes this important point when he says that these ministries must be ones of servant leadership rather than positional authority:

> The oft-designated "Ephesians 4:11 office ministries"—*apostles, prophets, evangelists, pastors, and teachers*—have been belabored in ways that have led me to resist the classic term "office ministries" frequently given them. This is because something *official* has increasingly drawn the focus away from Jesus' motive. His is the Giver of servant leaders, not the "elevator" of people to office or position.[1]

God calls individuals with specific fivefold leadership ministries to "equip the saints for the work of ministry" and encourage the body of Christ. There is nothing exalted about these gifts; they simply have a specific purpose and function to serve others.

Christ gave!

The gifts are not titles that are self-appointed or even chosen by the church. Rather, they are "given." Ephesians 4:11 says that "He gave." The fivefold gifts, from Jesus Christ Himself, were given so we might be complete, lacking nothing. Each of the gifts were fully functioning in Jesus when He walked this earth. He did not just carry a deposit of these gifts; each one of these gifts was functioning to its fullest extent in Christ. Jesus was all the fivefold ministers rolled up in one! Jesus was:

The Apostle of apostles "As the Father has sent me" (John 20:21).

The Prophet of prophets "At first His disciples did not understand all this" (John 12:16). Everything that Jesus prophesied will come to pass.

The Evangelist of evangelists "I am the way, the truth and the life; no man can come to the Father except through me" (John 14:6).

The Teacher of teachers "You call me Teacher and Lord and rightly so, for that is what I am" (John 13:13).

The Pastor of pastors "I am the Good Shepherd" (John 10:11).

All ministry is the ministry of Christ expressed through a believer by the anointing of the Holy Spirit. This includes the fivefold ministry which is an extension of the ministry of Christ Himself. There was no more an anointed apostle, prophet, evangelist, teacher, or pastor than Jesus Christ. He was all of these things and more.

When Jesus ascended on high He broke down His fullness of ministry into smaller measures. Christ in this way continues to carry on His prophetic ministry through the prophets He has set in the body. He continues to carry on His teaching ministry through the teachers that He has called and equipped in the body, and so forth.

His plan is to carry out a worldwide ministry through a many-member body.

If we want to see the church grow until we become like Christ, the five gifts are indispensable. When the fivefold is not working properly the church is handicapped. The modern day church is facing a challenge concerning how it views fivefold ministry, according to Doug Beacham. He believes that, although traditional denominations and the new apostolic networks do not see eye-to-eye when it comes to recognizing the fivefold ministers, they must work together to avoid the extremes of independence and institutionalism.

> Twentieth-century ... wineskins must be adapted to hold twenty-first century wine. I believe that apostolic and denominational leaders together hold the keys to adapting leadership structures so that the church can transform culture and advance the kingdom of God for generations to come.[2]

I agree wholeheartedly. We must work together and learn from each other even with our differing views. However, I cannot deny the operation of the fivefold gifts in the church today. I have seen them working firsthand. They are not lost. They did not disappear after the first century. These gifts have a vital role and purpose in the New Testament church just as they did in the book of Acts and the first three centuries of church history.

CHAPTER 3

The Purpose of Fivefold Ministers

"Go for the gold!" One of our church's fivefold ministers uses this favorite expression when encouraging people to reach out to their potential in God. It is his way of letting them know that the things of God are attainable if they give themselves wholeheartedly to the King and His kingdom. Jesus has already paid the price and forged the pathway for them to fulfill their destiny. As a fivefold minister, he knows his job is to train and encourage people to aim high.

Fivefold ministers have a burning desire to lead people into the fullness of their inheritance in Christ and the ministry to which He has called them. This "equipping of the saints" is accomplished as the fivefold ministers, who have been recognized as having a discernible and operative anointing in their gift, are also affirmed by their local church. They are called by the Lord and commissioned to work within and alongside the local church to help identify, acknowledge and stir up the various spiritual gifts within the body of Christ.

While these gifts do not automatically carry a governmental authority (the authority to rule or make governmental decisions to lead a church), they do carry a spiritual authority that cannot be denied. Their words and thoughts carry weight because of the gift and anointing in their lives. Those on a church leadership team having governmental authority respect and honor what the fivefold ministers are sensing, but they are the ones who make final decisions in relationship to the church they are leading. We will further address additional dynamics between church governing leadership and the fivefold ministers in the next chapter.

The fivefold gifts were given to the church to enable God's people to do the work of ministry. Effective fivefold ministers not only equip the saints for the work of ministry, but also help bring the body of Christ to maturity, according to Ephesians 4:11-12. Their goal as fivefold ministers is to train, equip and prepare believers to be functional in everyday life as ministers of the gospel of Jesus Christ so they can become mature spiritually. In other words, the fivefold ministry's job description is to enable believers to "walk the walk," not just "talk the talk." Their passion is to see the church come out of immaturity and into maturity.

The power of the five working together

We all have different roles to fulfill in the church. The gifts are intended for the good of the church so that His kingdom can be advanced. The fivefold individuals have grace given to them to qualify them for ministry as apostles, prophets, evangelists, pastors or teachers. The apostle brings the revelation of God's plan, the prophet brings the revelation of God's voice, the evangelist brings the revelation of God's mission to save souls and reconciliation, the pastor brings the sense of the love of God into the body, and the teacher brings the revelation of His Word.

Jesus desires each of these gifts to function in the local church so that every area of church life is strengthened and every individual becomes strong in Him. Each one of these fivefold gift individuals will look at things from a different perspective.

I have found that an easy and effective way to remember each of the fivefold gifts is by using our five fingers to symbolically represent the fivefold ministry. We could say the index finger is the prophet—he points in the direction the Lord is speaking to go.

The middle finger is the evangelist—out front bringing others to Christ. The ring finger is the pastor—the one who is married to the church. The little finger represents the teacher—who is able to probe into the truths of the Word of God. The thumb represents the apostle—he is the one who can touch all of the other four gifts. In Chapter 6, we will discover how the apostle brings unity to all the fivefold ministers and causes them to work together so that the church can move forward in oneness.

The power of all five working together packs a wallop! For example, if someone hit you with one or two of his fingers it may hurt a little bit. If he slapped you with all four of his fingers it would hurt quite a bit. But if he placed his four fingers together as one, using his thumb to anchor them into a fist and connect with you, his punch has the possibility of doing serious damage.

The same is true in the Spirit. When each of the fivefold gifts functions and flows together in unity with the apostolic touching each one, helping to give oversight and direction, there is a force that is released that knocks down the spiritual powers of darkness!

A divine tension

There is divine tension among the gifts. This is a good tension that happens when the five gifts are working together harmoniously. To illustrate, here are two very different perspectives a prophet and teacher have of the same Sunday service. The prophet says, "We should have spent more time in the presence of the Lord this morning. I felt the Lord was just about ready to speak and say something powerful to us. We should have worshiped a little bit longer. People were just beginning to respond."

The teacher says, "Why did we spend so much time in worship today? We are cheating the people out of the Word. They need to get more of the Word of God in them."

The divine tension between an evangelist and a pastor may sound like this: The evangelist says, "Let's just get more people saved."

The pastor counters, "We need to get those who are saved grounded in the Word of God. We can't handle more new babies."

The evangelist replies, "But they're already saved; we need to be concerned about those who aren't saved."

This divine tension between the gifts is a healthy one, but it takes someone with an apostolic gift to be able to draw from each of these gifts, bring them into unity and help them move forward with spiritual force.

The timeframe of the fivefold ministry

Very often in today's church when the subject of fivefold gifts is discussed there is much confusion. People ask, "How important is the fivefold? Are these gifts really for today?" Some say the five-fold ministry, especially the apostolic and prophetic ministry, passed away at the end of the first century. They believe that the fivefold ministry gifts are obsolete and are now lost to the church.

Some groups, believing that there are no apostles after the original twelve, call them the "fourfold" ministry gifts and acknowledge only the pastor, teacher, prophet and evangelist. Others think that the pastor-teacher is one gift—also having a "fourfold ministry" understanding. Still others feel the apostle is all four gifts rolled up as one, and that is what makes him an apostle.

How did the church become so confused over the fivefold ministers? Certainly, the New Testament church had a clear understanding of the fivefold ministry. However, with the passing of time, these ministries in the everyday life of the church became less clear, according to Vinson Synan, Dean and Professor of Divinity at Regent University:

> Thus, for centuries, the offices of pastor and teacher have been familiar ministries in all churches. However, only since the middle of the nineteenth century, with the success of Charles Finney and other "professional" evangelists of that day, has the office of evangelist gained a popular understanding and acceptance.

The offices of apostle and prophet have been more elusive for modern Christians. Many have accepted a belief developed throughout the centuries that the age of the apostles and prophets ended around 96 A.D., about the time John, the last apostle, died.... Over time, as the bishops consolidated their power in the church, the office of apostle was almost forgotten.[1]

In spite of the fact that the church ignored many aspects of the fivefold ministry down through the ages, I believe the operational timeframe for all of the fivefold ministers remains the same as the timeframe we see in Ephesians 4:13, "until we all reach unity in the faith and in the knowledge of the Son of God and become mature, attaining to the whole measure of the fullness of Christ."

Has the church reached "true unity in the faith"? Has it become fully spiritually mature "to the whole measure of the fullness of Christ"? With the many things that so often divide us, the church obviously has not completed its mission yet. The church still has much to accomplish, and all of the fivefold ministers should be in place to help us do it. They have been provided by Jesus so that we can be equipped to fulfill His mission that He gave us to do.

The fivefold gifts have been given to the church until the purpose laid out in Ephesians 4 is fully accomplished. Christ gave the gifts, so they will function until His return. From the time we are born until we go to be with Jesus, we need the impartation of the fivefold ministers. Their gifts are needed today more than ever. They were not meant to pass away with the death of the early apostles and prophets but to continue to the present age to help the body of Christ mature in unity. We desperately need the fivefold ministers with their gifts to help us come into the fullness of Christ.

It's a joint effort

Often today, many leaders and believers alike are under a misconception that all teaching, training and spiritual feeding for the congregation must come from the senior leader of the church. This way of thinking is cutting off all the help God has given the local church.

The senior leader of a church is responsible to see that the fivefold ministers are released in the church so that all believers can come to the unity of the faith. The goal is for the whole congregation to grow in maturity and faith and not be swayed by everything that comes down the Christian pipeline. The fivefold ministers help to ground believers in the Word of God and become more like Christ. Christ has provided teachers to help with the line upon line teaching, prophets to declare a word prophetically to assist in helping the congregation hear what the Lord is saying and evangelists to stir up the people and give them a heart for the lost.

With the fivefold ministry working together, God's divine intent is that no one person has to feel the weight of doing all the work on his own. Instead, a fivefold team of individuals can walk and labor alongside local church leadership to assist them in building the kingdom and helping to bring the saints to maturity. It is the way the Lord designed His church to function for it to come to maturity and stability.

Perhaps the church has had difficulty in releasing the fivefold ministers partly because Satan uses every device possible to prevent the fivefold operation in the church. He knows the power that would be unleashed if these individuals were released in their fullness.

I've heard one teacher say that if Satan can hijack these gifts, it will be as effective as the Philistines removing the blacksmiths from Israel which resulted in warriors without weapons. The enemy can restrain full operation of the fivefold by duping people into thinking they can manage without the gifts or otherwise confuse their understanding of the fivefold ministry.

In our family of churches, DOVE International, we have seen the fivefold released to a certain degree, but it hasn't been without difficulty. Yet, every time I read Ephesians 4, I am convinced that this is the way the Lord designed His church to function, and I am willing to do what is necessary to bring it about.

When we see the fivefold integrated and walking alongside the local church, I believe we will see a mature and powerful church released that will pull people out of the darkness of hell and turn them into future residents of heaven.

CHAPTER 4

What Do the Fivefold Ministers Do?

Fivefold ministers are trainers, equippers and builders. They train believers, ground them in the Word of God, equip them for ministry and build the kingdom of God. They do not build to be successful in their own ministries, but they build to see others become successful.

In the area where I live, there are many successful builders. What do builders do? They build for others. If you want a house built, a builder does not say, "Let me build your house so that you can help me become a successful businessman."

No, a builder says, "Let me build a house exactly the way you want it." In turn, the builder is building a successful business for himself.

Fivefold ministers serve the local church

A true fivefold minister builds for others. He works alongside a local church leader and offers his services by helping him construct what the Holy Spirit is building at that particular church. When a fivefold minister has a servant-like attitude, he is more likely to be accepted by the church leader and his team. In turn, the fivefold minister's need for affirmation and accountability is provided by the church leader and his team.

Sometimes a church leader tries to be "Superman" and embody all of the fivefold ministry gifts himself. The struggle this produces leads to ineffectiveness and isolation as he tries to compete with other ministry gifts. If a church leader does not understand that Jesus gave the fivefold ministry to assist him, he feels it is his sole responsibility to feed, train and equip the congregation. Although it is the church leader's responsibility to see that it happens, he certainly is not required to do all the equipping himself. Jesus provides anointed fivefold ministers to walk alongside the leader and his team to assist them in that process. When this is grasped, it is a great blessing to the leadership of a church.

Fivefold ministers derive their authority from Jesus

Fivefold ministers are secure in who they are. Their identity is in Christ, not their ministry. Paul, the apostle, realized that before he was a Christian, he endeavored to act in a certain way to gain the favor of people, but later, his higher aim was to please God and have His approval. "Am I now trying to win the approval of men, or of God? Or am I trying to please men? If I were still trying to please men, I would not be a servant of Christ."[1] Paul knew his security had to come from fulfilling God's plans and purposes for his life. Likewise, fivefold ministers derive their authority from God, not from those around them.

Fivefold ministers equip and encourage believers

There are two duties of the fivefold ministers. Fivefold ministers *equip* the saints for the work of ministry and *encourage* the body of Christ for that work. They must do more than preach good sermons. People will be changed and equipped through their ministry. For example, fivefold evangelists do not stop with training and inspiring people to evangelize; they also identify those who have an evangelistic call and help bring these gifts of evangelism to maturity.

The job of equipping and encouraging the gifts of believers to grow to maturity is quite a task and responsibility. This is why it requires fivefold ministers who are mature and seasoned—men and women who have a history with God. Bringing others to maturity is high priority for the fivefold ministry. Their heart's desire is that "... all attain to the unity of the faith, and of the knowledge of the Son of God, to a mature man, to the measure of the stature which belongs to the fullness of Christ."[2]

Fivefold ministers are "proven"

What is a *proven* ministry? It means fivefold ministers carry the ability to train and release others of like gifts and callings, and their local church leadership recognizes this ability. The Lord cannot trust them in a broader sphere of ministry if they cannot be trusted in their local church.[3]

A proven fivefold minister has the ability to activate a gift in others. He can mentor that gift and bring it to maturity, and then release that person into ministry, not feeling threatened by him, but encouraging the individual to go far beyond what he himself has. A proven fivefold minister speaks with the Lord's authority, and there is spiritual fruit, changed lives and signs following his ministry. In this way, Jesus validates those whom He has placed in fivefold leadership and ministry.

Many people have one or more of the fivefold gifts in seed form and yet are not considered proven fivefold ministers. They may potentially have a fivefold ministry gift but do not yet function in the full scope and authority of that gift. For example, someone may be an evangelist at his workplace and see many people come to know Christ, but that does not mean he is a fully developed fivefold evangelist. He has a fivefold gift in "seed form"[4] that is presently being developed.

In other words, a person can be a tremendous evangelist but if he is not able to do the five things listed below, he simply has an evangelistic gift; he is not a proven fivefold minister. A proven fivefold minister can do the following five things:

1. Has a discernible gift that is presently functioning

2. Can identify those who have the same gift

3. Can activate the gift and the individual

4. Can nurture and mentor the gift in others

5. Can release an individual into ministry

When a fivefold minister is *proven*, he and his ministry will be recognized as having a noticeable anointing (the power and presence of Jesus) and be affirmed by other fivefold ministers and apostolic church leaders. A proven fivefold minister, representing one of the ministry gifts of Jesus Christ, can function similarly to the "circuit rider" in early Methodism, ministering from church to church and small group to small group. At this point, he has a clearly defined ministry that has an impact on the church as a whole. His ministry becomes wider than one local church, and becomes "translocal."

At this point, it is worth noting the importance of character with regard to fivefold ministers. Character is a qualifier for those in a place of position or authority, although the Lord can use any-one to speak His Word and bring about a greater revelation. Jesus was with His disciples three years, and in those three years, their character and gifts were developed so that they were able to be the foundation layers of the New Testament church. Character is not a qualifier for discipleship, but it is a qualifier for leadership. For more on the character of fivefold ministers, see Chapter 12, which describes their qualifications.

The modern day struggles of releasing fivefold ministry

In the past few years, I have been given the responsibility of helping to see fivefold ministry released in our particular family of churches. I encourage the fivefold ministers to use their gifts by teaching and preaching at seminars and at other venues. It has not been without a struggle.

After months of encouraging our fivefold ministers to utilize their gifts, a fivefold minister from one of our churches finally took up the baton and planned a six-week course on prophetic ministry. On the first night of the course, he got extremely sick. He was able to conduct the course but dealt with severe pain and had to have three subsequent operations.

Within a four-month period, two of our other fivefold ministers required back operations. Yet another fivefold evangelist severely injured his knee while playing basketball with some youth. I believe this shows us that we must better understand the spiritual attack that comes against fivefold ministers and also that we need to more effectively cover them in prayer. The enemy is determined to sabotage the release of the fivefold because he knows the power that is unleashed through these ministries.

Another time, a group of our fivefold ministers wrote and planned a training seminar, but only one church in our network of churches used it. Sometimes the problem lies with the simple matter of church leaders not seeing the significance of fivefold ministry.

One reason some church leaders hesitate to utilize the fivefold ministers is that they have been disappointed by them. Often their disappointment comes from giving a platform to a fivefold minister, but the minister comes with his own agenda to build his own personal ministry rather than to serve the leader. This may be one reason why there has been a resistance to seeing the fivefold minister released on a full-scale level.

I have heard stories of fivefold ministers who were asked to come in and speak on a specific topic to strengthen an area in the church. However, when they came, they ministered something else of their own choosing. Maybe it was something that was more exciting to them, something that would make them look better in the eyes of the people, or something that could generate a larger love offering. Regardless of their reasons, the bottom line is that they did not follow through on what they were asked to do. Sadly, this shows the lack of maturity of the fivefold minister and puts obstacles in the way of his success.

One pastor told me in no uncertain terms that he would no longer allow a particular fivefold minister to speak at his church again. Apparently, he asked the individual to speak on a certain subject because the church needed help in that area. The date was set and the day arrived for the congregation to be taught on the topic agreed upon earlier. But on the day of training, the fivefold minister said he felt the Lord wanted to minister something else that day and proceeded to speak on another topic totally disregarding the pastor's desires. After this happened with the same individual a number of times, the pastor simply said, "I won't have him in to speak anymore because I can't trust him."

Although a fivefold minister has a burning passion to follow the leading of the Holy Spirit, he is dishonoring authority when he changes the topic without consulting the church leadership. The Lord often stirs a specific topic in a fivefold minister's heart and because it is in the forefront of his mind and spirit, it is hard to think that something else could be more important. Nevertheless, fivefold ministers need to honor the authority that has invited them and trust that authority's judgment on the present needs. Fivefold ministers are called to honor and serve the local church.

They also honor "time commitments" when they minister in the church. While there are times the Holy Spirit moves powerfully and ministry goes far beyond a given timeframe, it should be extended only with the affirmation of those in leadership. I have talked to senior pastors who have given the fivefold minister a timeframe, and to their disappointment they speak thirty minutes or longer beyond the allotted time. This is disrespectful to church leadership and also may hinder the individual from ever being invited again.

I always try to honor timeframes when I speak. If I see that I am running behind schedule, I will ask the leader in charge exactly when he wants me to close. I believe that if the power and presence of Jesus is there, the Holy Spirit will move on the leader's heart to give the amount of time necessary to accomplish what He wants to accomplish. Those who feel too restricted with timeframes are sometimes just unorganized and undisciplined in their preparation. I've heard the following story of one such hapless individual who went far beyond his allotted speaking time. The leaders in charge were using time cards to show when his time was running out because there were other speakers present, and a strict schedule needed to be adhered to in order for everyone to have an opportunity to speak. This particular individual just kept going on and on. A card was held up that said "stop." He kept going. The one with the time cards finally stood up and waved the cards thinking that the speaker had not seen him. The speaker kept speaking. Finally the only way to stop him was to turn the sound off! Talk about arrogance. What are his chances of ever being invited back again?

When a fivefold minister accepts his role and responsibility, he realizes that it is not about building his own ministry. He is assisting a church leadership team and co-laboring with the Holy Spirit in what God is doing in that local church. When he does that, there is a powerful dynamic released. In this way, the fivefold minister speaks from his anointing and strength. In addition, the body is trained and equipped, strengthened and anchored in the Word of God and grounded so it will not be tossed to and fro by every wind of doctrine.

If a fivefold minister leads a church, he must have an anointing for governmental leadership

While all fivefold ministers carry spiritual authority, not all fivefold ministers carry governmental authority. They may have a tremendous anointing of spiritual authority, and church leaders honor and respect what they are saying, but they never have a church governing leadership role. On the other hand, some fivefold ministers will provide governing leadership such as a pastor leading a local church or an apostolic position of leadership in a family of churches.

If you take into consideration the gift of leadership that is mentioned in Romans 12:8 ("if it is leadership, let him govern diligently"), a fivefold minister can hold governmental leadership but also must have the gift of government to lead or he will be out of place on a church leadership team. I have seen men and women who were tremendously anointed in their fivefold gifts and subsequently given governing leadership in the church. However, their anointing was not for government and they did not have the grace to deal with all the problems that came with church leadership. They simply could not handle it, and they eventually realized that governing leadership was not for them.

For the sake of example, let's say an evangelist and prophet are added to a church's leadership team. They do not have the gift to rule and become frustrated at the church leadership meetings because, to them, the meetings are a waste of their time. They think, "Instead of planning a budget, let's just believe God and go for it! There are people who are not saved so why are we spending time talking about the requirements for worship leaders, small group leaders, or whether we need to buy new chairs?" The person becomes distant during the meetings, leading to sometimes skewed and reactionary input. Those who do not have the gift of leadership cannot see the whole picture. They can only look at the issues through their *gift lens*.

What was once a church leadership team that was moving forward now is indecisive in decision-making. The leaders who were truly called to lead may start to feel as if they need to step down because they always seemed to be at odds with the fivefold evangelist and prophet. Before the leadership team is split apart, the leaders with the gift of government realize what needs to be done and wisely remove the evangelist and prophet from the church leadership team.

If someone has the fivefold gift of a pastor, it does not mean he has to be the primary leader of a church (having a governing role). Of course, the primary leader may have the fivefold gift of a pastor, but he must, first and foremost, have a governmental gift to lead and make final decisions. Likewise, a person with the fivefold gift of an evangelist may lead a church if he also has the gift of government. But if the evangelist does not have the gift of government, it will not work on a long-term basis. Anyone who leads a church must have the gift of governmental leadership that qualifies him to make final decisions.

Let's say for instance that Billy Graham walks into Christian Community Church and volunteers to preach the morning sermon. Mr. Graham, of course, has an amazing evangelistic anointing and carries tremendous spiritual authority. Still, he holds no governmental authority at Christian Community, so he will defer to the local leaders of Christian Community regarding what will take place at their morning worship service. These governmental leaders have the authority at their church to make final decisions.

This is true whether you have a ten-member house church or a 10,000 member mega-church. Someone has governmental leadership and is responsible to make the final decision.

Different levels of fivefold ministry

All the fivefold gifts have a sphere of ministry on the basis of relationship. Some are local, some are national and some are international. Fivefold ministry is always through relationship, not structure.

Local church—This is the first level of fivefold ministry. A local church leader and leadership team will identify and release individuals into their ministry gifts for that local congregation. Their sphere of ministry is within that particular church. In Acts, the local church in Antioch listed the prophets and teachers responsible for that church sphere. "In the church at Antioch there were prophets and teachers: Barnabas, Simeon called Niger, Lucius of Cyrene, Manaen...and Saul."[5]

Here is how it works in a local church setting. I pastored a local church for twelve years, and in that time released a number of fivefold ministers in the congregation in the following way. Let's say the church leaders notice that Mark is speaking God's thoughts prophetically. They watch him closely for a number of months and observe that he meets the qualifications and requirements and has a true heart to see people equipped, trained and released to minister.

The leadership team then communicates with Mark what they are sensing, and both Mark and his wife acknowledge his gift. The team then brings Mark before the congregation affirming his gift. Consequently, Mark receives a stamp of approval from the leadership team to travel freely throughout the congregation and small groups ministering in his prophetic gift. Mark's accountability, for his family and for the ministry, is to the local leadership team, because they are the ones that released him. If Mark makes a mistake in ministry, the local leadership team has the authority and the anointing to bring correction and adjustment to Mark. The confirmation of the fivefold minister is a sign of mutual accountability between the church and its chosen representative.

Family (network) of churches—This is the next sphere of development for a fivefold minister. When a local church leader and leadership team discern that the gift and anointing of an individual has grown beyond the scope of the local congregation, they recommend him to the next level of authority (the apostolic leadership of their family of churches), to be commissioned and released as a *translocal minister*. The term *translocal* refers to a fivefold minister who has the authority to travel from congregation to congregation in his network of churches to train, equip and release the saints for the work of ministry.[6]

The church leaders say, "Mark has really been faithful in training others and multiplying himself. We believe his gift goes beyond this local church to minister in our network of churches—those churches affiliated with ours."

The local church leader would then contact the leadership team of the network of churches, sharing what their local team is sensing. The leadership team of the network would also enter the discernment process to see if Mark is ready. Once affirmed, they would commission Mark as a prophet to their network of churches. He now has the stamp of approval to travel freely throughout the family of churches ministering prophetically.

Accountability for his ministry is provided by the leadership team of the network of churches that commissioned him. Accountability for his family primarily comes from the local church, where he is an active member and vital part of church life. If Mark makes a mistake in ministry in one of the network churches, it is the leadership team of the network of churches that has the responsibility to deal with the problem.

If a network of churches is an international family, I recommend that you have fivefold individuals released in geographical regions who are accountable to regional leadership. In some cases these regions are *nations* or *groups of nations* depending on how the regions are established.

For example, in the DOVE International family, we have regions of the world where there are different apostolic teams giving oversight to the churches within that region. We have a USA region, a Canada region, an Africa region and so on. There are apostolic teams that give oversight to each of these regions. We have fivefold ministers from all over the world, so instead of having one grouping of fivefold ministers, we have fivefold ministers in each region. Those who are in the USA are acknowledged by the USA Apostolic Team as having a fivefold gift and given the platform to minister both in the USA and anywhere else in the DOVE family. But accountability for their ministry comes back to the regional team that affirmed them. A fivefold individual from the USA can minister in Africa, as many do, but if there is a problem or a situation that needs to be corrected, it is the USA team that deals with that issue. In this way, we can see more fivefold individuals released.

We used to have just one international acknowledgment process and every individual with a fivefold gift needed to be acknowledged by the International Apostolic Team, but that became cumbersome. We knew as an international team we didn't and couldn't have the relationship with every fivefold individual in every region, so we decided to develop it region by region. If the regional team releases someone into the fivefold ministry, he has authority and affirmation to minister anywhere in the DOVE family, with the accountability coming back to the regional team that released him.

The fivefold minister would still have the authority of traveling anywhere in the network regardless of the nation he is from, but accountability for his ministry is from the local region. It helps to keep things from becoming too large and bureaucratic and retains the needed relational aspect.

The whole body of Christ—To be released in this sphere, a translocal fivefold minister must carry the affirmation of the overseers of the family of churches as well as other translocal fivefold ministers in the body of Christ.

The network of church leaders realize that Mark has further matured. A leader outside the church family usually affirms this. Mark is now at a place where he has matured enough to be used throughout the church body, across "family" church lines. During this time Mark will probably develop his own ministry name and have a team around him—one that has developed a deep trust and respect for him, that loves him and supports him so that his ministry is fruitful. He may even have a board-directed ministry. By this time, he should have a team of intercessors in place praying for him, his family and the ministry.

Accountability for the ministry goes back to the leadership team of the network of churches that commissioned him. Accountability for his family still resides within the local church of which he is a vital part. His sphere of ministry now extends to the body of Christ, and he carries within himself the character, authority and signs that are recognized by the larger sphere, namely the body of Christ at large but he is still connected to a local church.[7]

It all starts at the small group level!

We must remember that the seed of these fivefold ministry gifts dwells in many of God's people at the small group level. This is where we can begin to exercise our spiritual gifts and minister to others. The small group is a safe environment for ministry. It is a place to learn how to use our gifts and to become better equipped in ministering to others. The small group level is basic ministry training for a fivefold minister.

CHAPTER 5

The Goals of the Fivefold Minister

While the fivefold minister's purpose is one of *equipping* the saints and *encouraging* the body of Christ, how he accomplishes it is much broader. His goal is to edify the body, unify the body, see the body conformed to the image of Christ, reconcile the body to the Word of God and prepare every believer to fulfill his God-given destiny.

Edification

Overall, the ministry of the fivefold is one of edification to the body of Christ. Fivefold ministers are encouragers. They love people and desire to see them obtain all that the Lord is calling them to do. They want to see believers encouraged and walking in victory.

Probably one of the most discouraging aspects for a fivefold minister is to see people with great potential settling for a good deal less. I have personally identified those with tremendous gifts, but they are only fulfilling a minute portion of what I believe they could. Sometimes it is a matter of fully surrendering themselves to the Lord's plan for their lives. Other times, they refuse to deal with troubling issues in their lives or they are discouraged with life. A fivefold minister will encourage people like this to press on.

The Bible advises us to encourage one another daily. Have you ever wondered why Paul tells us to do that? It's because we can easily get discouraged. The enemy is always trying to undermine Christians because if he can dishearten them, he can keep them from fulfilling their destiny.

> But encourage one another daily, as long as it is called Today, so that none of you may be hardened by sin's deceitfulness (Hebrews 3:13-14).

A fivefold minister will encourage people so that they do not become hardened to sin or settle for second best. Encouragement just flows out of them. They are optimistic because they have the heart of Jesus in them. They believe the best and encourage people to give their best. I like to interact with fivefold ministers because I am encouraged by them. A true evangelist makes me feel like I can evangelize; a prophet gives me courage to press on; a pastor reaffirms Christ's love for me and helps me know that I am going to make it. An apostle stirs my quest for life, and a teacher motivates me to dig in the Word for fresh revelation.

Unification

Another goal of fivefold ministers is to bring us to the "unity of the faith" according to Ephesians 4:13. In today's church, various church doctrines differ and are presented in a way that often leads to division.

The fivefold ministers have the assignment of bringing the church to a unity of faith in the midst of this apparent lack of unity. They are kingdom-minded individuals looking for areas that we can agree on rather than areas that bring disunity.

I travel quite frequently and constantly meet new people at the various churches where I speak. Within five minutes of talking to someone, I can usually discern some issues that I realize will separate us or issues that we can agree upon. I try to focus on things that bring us together. After trust is built, I may explore those ambiguous areas, but always in the context of learning from each other, not to have a debate to prove myself right.

One time I was invited to a church to conduct a seminar, and I took along another brother who was being trained to teach seminars and was also a developing fivefold minister in our family of churches. The pastor of the church where I was conducting the seminar picked us up at the airport. Enroute to his church, I began to ask questions concerning his spiritual background, what his spiritual journey has been and what he feels are important issues surrounding the current state of affairs within his local area. In discussions such as these, I can often discern some biblical issues that may be "hot topics" to the individual. Within a few minutes of this particular conversation, the pastor brought up the topic of "women in leadership." He was very clear that his church believed that a woman could not serve in leadership, not even as a small group leader.

At that point in time, I had two choices: I could try to convince him that I believed that a woman could lead a small group, or honor his leadership and talk about the greater need—that women must be fulfilled and have their specific needs met. I chose the latter. I was not going to resolve this church debate in a short ride from the airport anyway. We had a great conversation and time together as I focused on things that we could agree on—the unsaved, discipleship, prayer, worship and the body of Christ at large.

The seminar was going well until the young developing fivefold individual, whom I had brought along to do some of the teaching, made this statement, "Sometimes women make the best small group leaders." Inside I cringed and wanted to cry, "Foul!" You could sense the awkwardness in the spirit; after all he was in the car with me and had heard my conversation with the pastor. After he finished speaking, I brought a brief public correction to what he had shared. I said that we affirm the decision of the leadership in this church to have only men serve as small group leaders, while I also affirmed the church's desire that women be fulfilled and have their specific needs met. I talked later to the developing fivefold minister and explained why I said what I did. I encouraged him to go to the pastor and ask him for forgiveness for his statement. The pastor graciously accepted and the relationship was preserved.

Fivefold ministers must be mindful of the larger picture that not all Christians interpret the Bible exactly alike. This may seem like an impossible task, but it can be done through Christ as He works through the Holy Spirit in the lives of believers in churches of various theologies. Fivefold ministers have non-negotiables, but they also have the rest of the body in mind and try to "major on the major things" and not get snagged on the little things that so easily divide the body of Christ.

As Christians, we are exhorted to "keep the unity of the brethren" (Ephesians 4:3). I think what Paul is saying here is that we have unity in Christ when we get saved, and we should not allow our own petty ideology to bring disunity.

Conformation

Jesus was faced with just about every situation known to man, and He was able to deal with these issues in a redemptive way. Fivefold ministers help believers become conformed to Christ, so they begin to grasp how to handle life circumstances and situations in a manner that will build the kingdom. Fivefold ministers have the ability to speak in a way that brings the Lord's conviction to us, as believers, exposing areas in our lives where we are not conformed to the One who made us. They do it in a way that encourages us and causes us to desire *change*. Christ's desire and goal is that we all are conformed to Him.

Sometimes people never reach their full potential because they refuse to deal with issues in their lives. Take Moses as an example. Did Moses fulfill his God-given destiny? No! Although he was ordained of the Lord to take the children of Israel into the promised land, he was unable to do so because he refused to deal with anger in his life. He was only allowed to look into the promised land from the mountain; he was not able to fulfill his God-given call. God tried to deal with his anger on a number of occasions, even taking him to the desert for forty years. Even so, Moses' anger remained an area in which he struggled and refused to completely relinquish to God. Moses didn't lose favor with God, but he certainly didn't fulfill all that the Lord had planned for him to do.

Our sin usually does not keep the Lord from using us. Sin is not hard for the Lord to deal with. In fact, He dealt with our sin once and for all on the cross. The thing that most hinders us from fulfilling our destiny in God is our own unwillingness to deal with the issues in our lives—if you will—our independence. Instead of allowing the Lord to come into our lives and facing our sin head-on, we hold Him at arm's length hoping that we can fix it ourselves. "After all, this little sin will not keep me out of heaven," we tell ourselves.

As I heard one man say, "We pay doctors hundreds of dollars to tell us what's wrong, but we go to God and say, "Just tell me everything's going to be all right." Fivefold ministers help us to deal with those things in our lives that hold us back, so our hearts turn afresh to the Lord. They help us to reach a new level of maturity, as we conform to Christ, so that we can become fully equipped to handle any situation in life.

Reconciliation to the Word

A fivefold minister is not just concerned about your salvation, he is concerned that you obtain your full potential in God. And the only way that you will realize your potential is by being conformed to the Word. Fivefold ministers ground us in the Word so that we are not tossed to and fro by every wind of doctrine. The Word of the Lord is their plumb line, and they minister from that base of authority. They desire not only that we would be conformed to Jesus but that the Word of God be formed in us, so that the situations and circumstances in life do not spin us out of control.

Their goal is that we are grounded in the Word, ready to speak against every false doctrine, not easily fooled by cunning demonic or fleshy thoughts or ideas, growing and maturing in our relationship with Jesus and each other. For a fivefold minister, there is never a question on whether or not the Word is relevant. It is as relevant today as it was the day it was written. The fivefold minister's desire is that the Word would take preeminence in our lives and that our lives would be reconciled to the Word and the Author of it.

Fivefold ministers are able to teach and preach with authority. They know who they are in Christ, and they know and understand the Word of God. They know the authority of the Word of God and are able to stand on it allowing the Word to speak for itself. Their goal is to bring the church to maturity because a mature church is a strong church.

Preparation

Fivefold ministers have the goal of bringing us to the "measure of the stature which belongs to the fullness of Christ."[1] Their goal is to prepare us for ministry. When fivefold ministers contribute their gifts, believers receive an impartation so each one can be better equipped to fulfill God's call on his or her life.

The heart and desire of the fivefold minister is to expand the ministry of others. When they are ministering and see that the people are being changed and transformed, they become ecstatic.

When my friend Calvin, a prophetic-teacher, is teaching and sees that the Word is connecting in people's spirits, he gets more and more excited. As a fivefold teacher, his greatest desire is that people would grasp the same revelation that he has. When they do, he gets pumped up spiritually! Fivefold ministers love to see people growing in the Lord. It is what makes them tick. They want to see themselves multiplied.

Jesus was excited to leave earth because He knew that the Comforter would come and reside in the hearts of men. A fivefold minister's desire is to see others growing up in their full potential, prepared for life and all the circumstances that come their way. Jesus was never shaken by life circumstances but used every circumstance in life as an opportunity to minister God's heart and bring about change.

A fivefold minister is a catalyst

A fivefold minister has no desire to do all the ministry himself. His desire is to see others trained and equipped and released for the work of ministry. He enjoys watching others growing in God. He thrives on preparing others so that they, too, are able to minister to those around them on a daily basis. Fivefold ministers have a passion to see individuals take the church to the people. Their goal is not to just draw people around them, but to equip people who are around them and send them out into their own communities to minister to their family, friends, neighbors and people in their workplace.

A fivefold minister is not out to build his own ministry; he wants to build the body of Christ, equipping the saints for the work of ministry. In so doing, his ministry will be built, and he will experience the opportunity of being a catalyst in the lives of others.

Fivefold ministers model ministry

Sometimes fivefold ministers think they have grown beyond actually *doing* ministry and now they should just be involved in *equipping* or training others for ministry. Although fivefold ministers have the job of equipping the saints for ministry, they also continue to model ministry themselves. For example, evangelists should not be content to tell other people, in a church setting, how to evangelize; they should also be actively involved in bringing people to Jesus in their day-to-day life. In this way, they are modeling evangelistic ministry.

We normally think of the fivefold gifts as ones to be used to help believers, but fivefold ministers who model ministry in their daily lives will reach out to nonbelievers with their gifts. When you really think about it, wouldn't it be more important to tell the nonbeliever who sits beside us on an airplane what God has to say to him (prophesy over him) than to the person in the church who hears God on a regular basis?

God gave us these gifts to bring others into the kingdom. Five-fold ministers should be actively using their gifts to minister to those who do not know Him. Modeling ministry is just as important as teaching methodology or theology. Jesus not only taught His disciples what to do, He showed them how to do it.

In the following chapters, we will take a fresh look at how each of the fivefold ministers relates to the body of Christ. Here, in brief, are the descriptions of the fivefold ministers and their functions, as described by Dr. Bill Hamon:

> Apostles are like fathers and mothers who impart to the body of Christ and raise them up as sons and daughters in the faith. Prophets bring supernatural revelation and insight, giving vision of the times and seasons of God so that saints know what to do. Teachers teach the Word of God with simplicity and wisdom. Pastors nurture the body of Christ with counseling, clothing them with Christlike armor and garments. Evangelists impart zeal for souls to be saved and equip the saints with wisdom and anointing

CHAPTER 6

Apostles Govern

"You are going to be a pastor to pastors." There it was again—another prophetic word given to me by someone who didn't know who I was. This was not the first time this happened nor would it be the last. I was a young pastor just trying to do my best with the new church the Lord had planted and now He was saying that I would be a "pastor to pastors"—an apostolic leader. How was that going to happen? How could it be possible? I was struggling with the thought that I was not qualified to lead any group much less lead other pastors. I was just a dairy farmer turned pastor. Not so long ago my whole life had been focused around farming. What was this new thing called *apostolic* and how would I ever fit into it? It was the late 1980s, and this was new terminology for me.

While modern Christiandom has come to accept the ministry gifts of evangelists, pastors and teachers, the gift of apostle and gift of prophet have not been as widely accepted—especially the ministry of an apostle. Some would say this gift ended many centuries ago. This view mistakenly assumes that the role of the apostle was limited to the original twelve apostles chosen by Jesus. A careful reading of the New Testament will show otherwise. Let's take a look at the evidence.

Apostles mentioned in scripture

First of all, Jesus Christ is the chief apostle. "Therefore, holy brothers, who share in the heavenly calling, fix your thoughts on Jesus, the apostle and high priest whom we confess."[1]

The first apostles were prepared and sent out personally by Jesus. They were the twelve apostles who were unique eye-witnesses of the risen Lord and His ascension.[2] They had been trained by Jesus for the job and were chosen by Jesus to represent Him.

Then there were several post-ascension apostles—Andronicus, Junia, James, Barnabas, Titus, Epaphroditus, Timothy, Silvanus, Apollos, Titus, Paul, to name a few.[3]

These apostles were trained and sent out by the church. In other words, they studied and repeated what the first apostles taught. Jesus predicted that this would happen: He told the first twelve apostles, "...if they obeyed my teaching, they will obey yours also."[4]

Indeed, the second line of apostles had successfully repeated and obeyed what the first apostles taught. These apostles realized their unique authority as Jesus' representatives. They had followed the first apostles' teachings which were identical to Jesus' teachings. When Paul visited the brothers in Galatia, they welcomed him "as if [he] were Christ Jesus Himself."[5]

A biblical apostolic pattern

Tracing the steps of the apostles in the New Testament gives modern day apostles a biblical pattern to carry out their ministries. The first twelve apostles seem to have worked out of Jerusalem for several years, devoting their time to evangelizing the lost and teaching the new believers and occasionally taking short missionary trips.

By the time Paul arrived in Jerusalem, however, the first apostles seem to have left with only James remaining. It seems apparent that after the first initial years in Jerusalem, most of the first apostles moved around as itinerate leaders, stopping to preach the gospel and organize churches and then continuing on to new locations.

Paul spent some time in Corinth,[6] Ephesus[7] and Rome.[8] He instructed Timothy to "stay in Ephesus so that [he] might command certain men not to teach false doctrines any longer."[9] After that job was finished Paul told him to "do your best to get here before winter."[10] Similarly, Titus was left in Crete to "straighten out what was left unfinished and to appoint elders in every town."[11] After this was completed, Titus joined Paul at Nicopolis.[12]

Apostles have always been foundation layers and spiritual parents. They are parenting-type figures who have the ability to attract and birth other leaders. They are master builders who have a strong passion to see the church built on right foundations. They are servants of the church who are sent out by the church to evangelize and to plant churches, thus having an itinerant ministry as they often exercise general leadership over a group of churches.

Modern day apostles

We believe that God is raising up many modern day apostles who love His church and who serve as fathers and mothers in the body of Christ. These apostles have a desire to train and raise up church leaders to come to maturity, to release them, and then move on to plant another church. Their greatest joy is to reproduce themselves in their spiritual children as they parent them to adulthood.

Apostles are spiritual entrepreneurs who love change and relish finding new ways of doing things. They are always coming up with new concepts and new patterns. They are willing to take chances, and at the same time willing to change. They are not satisfied with "the way things are" but burn with a greater vision for the church.

They "prepare God's people for works of service"[13] as they are sent out with an apostolic anointing that flows through them to "send" every believer.

The word *apostle* comes from the Greek word *apostolos* which is translated *sent one* and carries the understanding that the one being sent has the full power and authority of the one sending him. He is sent by God with a mandate from the Lord Jesus to build, plant, nurture, correct and oversee His church. Apostles are called "wise master builders or spiritual architects."[14] They are foundation layers.[15] They have a desire to build something that did not exist before. I like Peter Wagner's description of a modern day apostle:

> The gift of apostle is the special ability that God gives to certain members of the body of Christ to assume and exercise general leadership over a number of churches with an extraordinary authority in spiritual matters, that is spontaneously recognized and appreciated by those churches. Apostles are those whom God had given especially to pastors and church leaders. They are those to whom pastors and church leaders can go for counsel and help. They are peacemakers, troubleshooters and problem solvers. They can make demands that may sound autocratic but that are gladly accepted because people recognize the gift and the authority it carries with it. They have the overall picture in focus and are not restricted in vision to the problems of one local church.[16]

An apostle develops his gift

The gift of apostle often develops over a period of years. An individual may begin in ministry in one of the other gifts—teacher or pastor, for example. During this time, his ministry is developed and proven with further gifts that may become evident along the way. An apostle understands ministry from personal experience.

With Paul, there was a seventeen-year period between his conversion and commissioning to be an apostle. Paul was acknowledged by the other apostles after considerable evidence to show that he was doing the work of the ministry in obedience to God's call.

Here's my personal story of developing as a grassroots apostolic leader. When I first became part of DOVE International, it was a fledgling small group-based church that patterned its structure after Paul Yonggi Cho's church in Korea. I joined a small group in my area, the only one in the county that I lived in, because DOVE was just starting to expand into my area.

Two years later, my small group leader moved to Kansas, and I became the new leader. I was out of my comfort zone, but the small group grew and multiplied into two groups. Since I was growing in my ability to lead, both my wife and I started to give oversight to the new small group as well as leading the original one. Both of these groups multiplied again. Before long, we were leading one small group and giving oversight to three.

The day came when there was talk of starting a new church in our county. Some people were driving an hour to a service every Sunday morning, but there was a vision to start one closer to where they lived. Since I was giving oversight to some of the small groups in the area, I was asked if I would be willing to serve on the team to help plant this new church. Months went by. Through much prayer and communication we planted a new church. A few months after the church was planted, I was asked to lead this new plant because the individual who was currently leading it was going to Brazil to become a missionary.

So, there I was—a farmer by day and a church planter by night! It took another five months until I made the final decision to sell the farm. It was one of the hardest decisions that I have ever made. I was now in what was considered "full-time in ministry." The truth is, I had always considered myself full time in ministry even while in the workplace. I had ministered to many people on the farm—employees, salesmen, bankers, accountants, neighbors and anyone else with whom I came in contact. One time I went to buy grain from a farmer and begin to talk to him about making Jesus the Lord of his life, and he did. God was moving, people were giving their hearts to the Lord, being set free of the demonic influences in their lives and living for Jesus. The small groups were growing, and the church was moving forward.

After it was prophesied a number of times, I began to warm to the idea that there may be somewhat of an apostolic call on my life—even though at the time I was still a young pastor, just trying to make sure that my church didn't fail!

Before long, I was asked to serve on the leadership team that gave oversight to the three congregations that comprised DOVE at the time. Then we had a vision to plant a church in another city, and since I had built a relationship with the potential senior elder, Mike, and because of my previous experience of giving oversight to a growing number of small groups, I was asked to assist Mike in planting the church in Elizabethtown. He was the new sub-district pastor and I met with him on a regular basis to help him establish the new church plant by providing discernment and problem solving. My apostolic gift was being tested and developed.

Authority comes from the Lord and is confirmed by others

An apostle is not self-appointed. He is chosen by the Lord himself. Peter Wagner agrees with this assessment: "There is no such thing as a true apostle who is self-appointed. God is the one who decides to whom He wishes to give the spiritual gift of apostle."[17]

An apostle's greatest responsibility is to the Lord who has called him. However, his call must be affirmed by those whom the Lord brings to him,[18] by other apostles, and by spiritual leaders in the body of Christ.[19]

An apostolic calling does not automatically mean that the apostle has the right to exercise authority. His authority is by invitation. The church leaders who look to him for apostolic oversight invite him into their realm. His apostleship is proven over time, and they trust his authority and leadership. Remember, apostles are foundation layers and releasers. Their goal is to see the local church succeed. They are not into controlling leaders: their ministry is one of giving advice that will lead to success. It is a ministry based upon relationship and exercised within a sphere of influence. In this manner the ministry of an apostle is evidenced by his call from the Lord, the commissioning of his local church, the leaders of his family of churches and the affirmation of other leaders within the body of Christ. Apostles help strengthen the local leadership.

Apostles are called to build and plant churches

Apostles have the ability to forge into new territory and take the gospel to unreached areas.[20] As an "architect" an apostle designs and lays foundations for new churches. They want new foundations to be built on Jesus Christ and His Word rather than human traditions and opinions.

Paul was commissioned by the Lord and by other apostles in the early church to build and to plant churches among the Gentiles.[21] Peter was commissioned by the Lord to build and to plant churches among the Jews.[22]

It seems that the authority of an apostle changed in nature once a local church was established and had the oversight of local elders. For example, Paul took on the role of a father whose authority diminished once his spiritual sons or daughters reached adulthood.

Beware of false apostles who steal what others have laid

With this new release of apostolic fathers will arrive false apostles. False apostles prey on the works and finances of others. Looking for churches already established and wanting to use those churches to enhance their portfolio, they say, "Come join me."

They have not labored to see these works established but instead are looking for what a church can bring to them versus the true apostolic mindset that says, "How can I help this church succeed?"

I tell our church leaders that our apostolic team exists for two reasons—to serve Jesus and to serve them as church leaders. If we stop doing either of these two things, we have lost our reason for existence.

False apostles are also destitute of supernatural manifestations and have no power in their ministry. Their own mouth gives the strongest witness of their apostleship.[23]

A true apostle has those who say, "If it were not for this person, I would not be successful in ministry." In 1 Corinthians 9:2, Paul told the Corinthians, "You are the seal of my apostleship." In other words, they were proof to the world that he had an apostolic gift functioning in his life because of the spiritual fruit of his labors among them.

Growing in apostolic ministry

My apostolic gift did not happen overnight. It started to function in my life as I gained more and more experience in pastoral ministry and also as my prophetic gift began to develop. I noticed the prophetic gift especially when I would be praying for people in my congregation. Often the Lord would give me a word of knowledge for someone while we were in prayer for a specific situation or there was a blockage in the healing process. I began to prophesy over people, and the words were accurate. I continued to exercise this gift all the while I was still pastoring the church.

When our church made the change from one local church with eight USA congregations to an international apostolic network of churches, it was a natural switch for me to be on the apostolic team because the Lord had been developing the apostolic gift in me for years. While we are very hesitant to use the term *apostle*—because we like to describe the work that the individual does more than giving him a title—we knew that there was a call on my life for apostolic ministry. By this time, there were a number of churches to which I was giving oversight. I was assisting them in vision casting, problem solving and ministry development.

Then as we continued to grow as an international movement, I was praying over the world map at our offices one day, and I felt the Lord say to me, "Take responsibility for the USA and release

Larry to the world." (Larry Kreider is the International Director of DOVE International). It was a clear word to me. I kept it to myself for awhile but later in meeting with Larry I mentioned my willingness to serve him in that capacity if the Lord confirmed it. It was a number of years later that it was confirmed, and today I give leadership to the apostolic team that gives oversight to the DOVE churches in the USA. I have never had to strive for a position in ministry. I stayed faithful in doing what the Lord placed in front of me and was willing to take the next step if and when He wanted me to. The Bible says "a man's gift makes room for him" (Proverbs 18:16). We need to stay faithful and available, and when that gift is needed the Lord will open the door and say, "Now it is time."

Apostles train leaders and problem solve

Training leaders is an important apostolic function. When Paul and Barnabas made their second visit to Lystra, Iconium and Antioch, they ordained elders in each church.[24] Appointing leaders of local churches should be the job of apostles working with the local leadership teams rather than a matter of congregational voting or other selection. (For more teaching on biblical church government, I recommend the manual *Helping You Build Cell Churches* or video training from our DOVE Leadership and Ministry School, available at www.dcfi.org).

Local churches often encounter problems that need outside assistance. Local leaders sometimes have blind spots that need the apostolic ability to break through the blindness and speak God's Word to areas of imbalance or division or other problems. Paul's first letter to the Corinthians illustrates his ability to use his apostolic authority to speak to the problems in the church.

One of the churches in our movement was having a real problem between an evangelist and the senior leader of the church. While I was visiting one time, the church leader asked if I would be willing to meet with them to help work out their relationship. As we met, the Lord gave me a fresh outside perspective that neither of them could see because they were in the thick of the situation. As the Lord gave insight, healing took place and the relationship was restored. Where there was once a deteriorating relationship, through the apostolic gift at work, there was now a healed relationship! Even today these two men are working together planting house churches. The church leader is a real spiritual father to the evangelist. This is how it is supposed to work.

How Paul-type and Timothy-type apostles work together

Although there are many different types of apostles mentioned in the early church, let's look briefly at the Paul-type apostle and Timothy-type apostle and their corresponding roles.

A Paul-type apostle is an overseeing apostle. This kind of apostle is sent by the Lord with a vision burning on his heart to establish a family of churches, and it will burn on his heart until he fulfills it. The blueprint and vision come from the Lord. His call is affirmed by other apostles and spiritual leaders in the body of Christ.[25] This kind of apostle has a burden to see God's people gather as a united force, and he also has the ability to sense the heartbeat of what the Lord is speaking to a particular family of churches.

An overseeing apostle gets his authority from the Lord,[26] and God equips him for this work, supplying him with the supernatural faith and perseverance to see this vision become a reality. The Lord brings others alongside an overseeing apostle to fill in what is lacking in his gifts so the vision can be fulfilled. Paul recognized that Peter was an apostle to the Jews, and he was called by God to build the church among the Gentiles. Additionally, a team of apostles served with him.[27]

In my own experience, there was a clear call to our apostolic leader, Larry Kreider, to lead our family of churches called DOVE International, and for others, like myself, to serve alongside him. There was more to do than he could ever accomplish himself, and he needed others so that he could be free to expand the ministry in other areas.

A Timothy-type apostle helps the Paul-type. The Timothy-type apostle is affirmed and commissioned to help fulfill the vision received by the Paul-type apostle from the Lord. He is sent out by the Paul-type apostle with specific instructions and mandates that will contribute to the main goal the Lord has given to the apostolic team. His field of ministry is limited to that which he was sent to do.[28] He is the father to the churches he plants.[29] His sphere of ministry is given to him by the Lord and by the overseeing (senior) apostle with whom he serves. Timothy and Titus were sent by Paul to establish elders and oversee churches.[30]

This is where my role comes into play within DOVE International. I was called to lead a local congregation, and as I, and the gifts the Lord gave me, continued to mature, my sphere of influence continued to grow. I was released as a Timothy-type apostle, and today I lead a team of apostolic leaders that gives oversight to our churches in the USA. That authority was given to me by Larry Kreider who as the international apostolic leader has the final responsibility for all of DOVE International.

The marks of an apostleship

The Corinthians were Paul's "seal" of his apostleship.[31] That is, they were the spiritual fruit of his labors among them. They were proof that God really "gave the increase." The proof is in the tangible results of changed lives. Also indicative of modern day apostles are supernatural signs, wonders, miracles and perseverance.[32] Those in apostolic authority should especially bear the credentials of demonstrating and imparting a supernatural dimension of the kingdom of God.

If we are to believe for the supernatural, the apostles should be leading the way, sharing vision and raising the expectation of the people that they serve, demonstrating the power of the Holy Spirit. Jesus, our apostle of apostles, came to preach the gospel of the kingdom and demonstrate the power of the kingdom. Apostles are to carry on that heritage.

An apostle normally carries a measure of the gifts of prophet, evangelist, pastor and teacher

Most apostles have been used by the Lord at some time in their lives and ministry in the ministry gifts of prophet, evangelist, pastor and teacher. They often are a gift mix. In other words, some five-fold ministers are prophetic teachers, others are pastoral teachers, others are apostolic evangelists. Paul was an apostle, a prophet and a teacher.[33]

As I look at my gift mix, there are a number of things that are clear. I have had a strong pastor gift, but in some ways that has lessened over the years, even though it is still evident in the way I think and minister. I also have a prophetic gift at work. I travel numerous times to minister prophetically in different venues, and the Lord is always faithful to provide prophetic insight and ministry to individuals and the church as a whole. While my prophetic gift is not as strong as some who are purely prophetic in their make-up, there is a discernible prophetic flow that comes out of me. Additionally, there is the apostolic gift that is affirmed by others to whom I give apostolic oversight.

The qualifications of an apostle

An apostle must have the character qualifications of those in church leadership.[34] Just as Christ, the Apostle, came with a servant's heart, a modern day apostle must have a servant's heart.[35] As a representative of Christ, an apostle must be clothed with humility.

Sent by Christ to do Christ's work,[36] an apostle must have a parent's heart. This means he has a desire to see his spiritual sons and daughters far exceed him in ministry.[37]

An apostle will have a heart to release others. Since his work is to build, he is not afraid to release others to the work of God. He sees others as helping to bring *completion* not *competition* to the ministry the Lord is building.[38]

An apostle will be someone whom other leaders will want to emulate and serve and follow.[39] An apostle is willing to sacrificially suffer for the church.[40] As a father, he gives no thought to himself, but is concerned only that the vision of God advances.

Apostles move the other gifts forward

Remember how we said that the thumb is symbolic of the apostle? The thumb is the driving force that can be powerful when curled into a fist using the other four fingers. If the apostolic gift rises to its place of power and function bringing the other gifts together, a deafening blow can be dealt to the spiritual powers of darkness.

The apostolic gift is needed to bring the best out of the other four gifts. In Chapter 3, we mentioned the divine tension that is present in the spiritual realm between the different gifts. Because of this divine tension, it requires the apostle in the center to see the whole picture in order to take what the teacher, prophet, evangelist, pastor is saying and move forward. Otherwise, the tension may instead cause the other gifts to work against each other.

God has created the apostolic gift to help move the other gifts forward successfully. An apostle has the God-given ability to walk with the prophet, evangelist, pastor and teacher, drawing them together with a common vision and purpose.

Apostles and prophets, especially, are called to work together

It is essential for modern day apostles to have proven prophets working alongside them.[41] Together they form a powerful team if they learn to honor each other's gifts and work together. The apostle keeps the church in a forward thrust, and the prophet helps the apostle to see the current "word of the Lord" so he is building properly.[42] The prophetic also keeps the apostle on track and true to the call of the Lord on his life. The apostle and prophet not only complement each other by working together in the unity of the Spirit, but they also need each other for the enhancement of each of their ministries.

Most apostles are aware of how much they need the prophetic, but not all prophets are aware of how much they need the apostolic in their lives. Without the apostle, the prophet can begin to think more highly of himself than he should, for he carries the "word of the Lord." The apostle is able to speak to the prophet and bring correction and adjustment where necessary. The apostles need the prophets, or they will have a tendency to miss some very important things that the prophets can see.

There have been a number of times when, as apostolic leaders, we have a real sense of the direction we should go, but the prophets help to show us some key things that are missing before we can advance to where we want to go. Sometimes it is an aspect of timing or something that is specifically hindering us from moving forward. The prophetic gift brings it to the light so that we can deal with it effectively. When we knew that the Lord wanted us to purchase our own property for a headquarters for our family of churches, the apostolic ministers found a place. Before we were willing to make any final decisions, however, we brought some prophets to the building to see if they sensed the "go ahead." They did, and today we own the property.

Sometimes individuals who have both an apostolic and a prophetic gift will find themselves in the following scenario. When they are around someone with a strong apostolic gift with the apostolic authority for a given area, their prophetic gift is much stronger. And when they are around someone with a stronger prophetic gift where they have the apostolic authority, they operate in a much stronger apostolic gift. It's part of the Holy Spirit's ability to draw out what is necessary where it is needed.

I find this especially true for me when I am ministering alongside a strong apostolic gift that has authority. When my colleague Larry and I minister together, his strong apostolic gift functions and I find myself operating in a much stronger prophetic role. This doesn't happen every time but often enough for both of us to notice it.

Likewise, when I am in a setting where I am the apostolic authority and there is another prophetic gift present, I do not function nearly as much prophetically.

To learn more about apostolic ministry, I recommend a DVD training series on "Modern Day Apostles" available at www.dcfi.org.

CHAPTER 7

Prophets Guide

Some time ago, I invited a good friend and established prophet, Dennis, to come and minister to the fivefold ministers in our family of churches. Dennis is a fun-loving, practical sort of guy who is a real father in the prophetic. As he started to share with us, he related this dialogue that occurred between two prophetic individuals.

Two prophets were walking toward each other. The one stuck out his hand and said, "I see that you're doing okay; how am I doing?"

This humorous interaction communicates how prophets tend to hear from the Lord for others better than they hear for themselves!

One of the best definitions of a prophet I've come across is "Someone who sees what others do not, who hears what others cannot, who speaks what others will not." A prophet is someone who has the ability to consistently speak forth God's heart to His people. The prophet sees the real issues and priorities. He calls us to action and points the way. A prophet is one who speaks forth God's heart and mind maturely and who has a proven record of accuracy.

We are admonished by the scriptures to seek the prophetic word of the Lord. The Bible tells us in Matthew 10:41 that if we welcome a prophet and receive him, we will receive a prophet's reward. This is saying, at the very least, that if we are open to the prophetic gift, we will receive a blessing from God.

The prophet is an extremely important gift, especially in the way it relates to the apostolic gift in helping to lay a foundation for churches to build and to expand according to Ephesians 2:19-20.

Consequently, you are no longer foreigners and aliens, but fellow citizens with God's people and members of God's household, built on the foundation of the apostles and prophets, with Christ Jesus himself as the chief cornerstone.

Prophets are in place in the church to bring supernatural revelation and insight so that believers can receive direction from the Lord. Amos 3:7 says, "The sovereign Lord does nothing without revealing His plans to His servants the prophets." A prophet sees the picture through God's eyes and helps to open up our hearts to hear God.

My own prophetic gift has grown over the years from speaking prophetic words to small groups to traveling to other states and nations and ministering to people using the gift mix that the Lord has given me. Recently, I returned home from Bulgaria where I and another leader ministered prophetically over the leaders at their leadership meetings. Another night we were in another city teaching and ministering prophetically over a small group.

I have had the opportunity to take prophetic teams into businesses to give prophetic insight for their future development and expansion, not knowing anything about them or their business. There have been times where I have been praying for someone or for their business and the Lord has given me something to share with them. Sometimes it is a warning or an encouraging word. One time I was praying for a particular business, and I felt the Lord say immediately, "Full court press." I passed this on to the business owner, and he told me he was struggling with a particular deal and was wondering if he should continue. The word assured him to press on, and he was able to accomplish what he felt the Lord was speaking to him. I believe there is a whole aspect of prophetic ministry that the Lord wants to develop to assist businessmen and help them become more successful so that more finances can be poured into the kingdom and the work of the kingdom.

Sometimes I am invited to a leaders' retreat with the sole purpose of ministering prophetically over the leaders. These are some examples of the prophetic gift at work in my life as I have tried to be faithful with the gifts that the Lord has given.

Comparing Old Testament and New Testament prophets

The Lord spoke to His people in the Old Testament through the prophets. They needed to be infallible in their ministry (if their words did not come true, they were stoned) and they were used to give direction and guidance to God's people.

While the Old Testament prophets were the direct mouthpieces of God, today they are often used to confirm the word the Lord is speaking to the hearts of individuals.[1] They may also be used by the Lord to ignite a vision or calling in an individual.

This must be confirmed by the witness of the Holy Spirit in an individual's own life and/or the affirmation of his church leadership. Every believer has an "anointing from the Holy One" and can hear from God.[2]

If someone gives me a word and it does not bear witness with the Holy Spirit within me, I put the word on the shelf, so to speak, and leave it there. If it is from the Lord, it will come to pass at a later time, or if there is more revelation that I need the Lord will provide it.

Part of the nature of the prophet is that he will not only confirm what God has spoken to us but also take us into the realm that will stretch us by calling us to deeper things. We do not just follow the prophetic word but the witness of the Holy Spirit in our hearts. God enables His thoughts to be clearly verbalized through a Spirit-inspired person, according to an author and individual who is active in prophetic conferences worldwide. His definition of prophecy is

> God shares His thoughts about a given situation by inspiring one of His Spirit-filled servants to speak these thoughts to the appropriate person or persons in understandable language and in the power of the Holy Spirit.[3]

We must remember that it is the written Word of God, the Bible, that is our plumb line. Every word must measure up to the Word of God. If someone gives me a prophetic word that is contrary to the Word of God, I throw it out. I know it is not from the Lord because He will not contradict His written Word.

The Bible is clear that we should be willing to die for the written Word of the Lord but not the prophetic word. However, scripture does tell us in 1 Timothy 1:18 to wage the good warfare according to the prophetic words that have been spoken over us. We must endeavor to secure the victory for the prophetic word to see it become a reality, but it is only the written word of the Lord that we lay our lives down for.

Prophets in the Old Testament

If we compare the ministry of prophets under the Old and New Covenant, we see a number of differences.

The Holy Spirit came upon them.

Frequently they were used to give warning and foresight.

Those who were in authority used prophets to hear from the Lord for direction.

Often their prophecies also had a demonstration with the Word.

They called people to repentance.

They most often were alone and living away from other people.

They were feared by both the average person and the one in authority.

They spoke of Messiah coming.

Prophets in the New Testament

They call people to embrace the provisions of the new covenant by entering into a relationship with Jesus Christ.

The Holy Spirit lives within them.

They often affirm what the Holy Spirit has already been speaking to people.

They equip people to hear from God for themselves.

They declare that Jesus Christ is here and has provided all that is necessary.

They mingle among the people.

They use their gifts to expose the works of darkness.

They desire to bring the body to maturity and unity.

"Another world" prophets

Sometimes prophets tend to look at life from a seemingly mystical viewpoint and forget to be practical. It reminds me of the story told of Sherlock Holmes and Dr. Watson on a camping trip. After a good meal they were exhausted and went to sleep.

Some hours later, Holmes awoke and nudged his faithful friend. "Watson, look up at the sky and tell me what you see."

Watson replied, "I see millions and millions of stars."

"What does that tell you?"

Watson pondered for a minute. "Astronomically, it tells me that there are millions of galaxies and potentially billions of planets. Astrologically, I observe that Saturn is in our Galaxy. Time wise, I deduce that it is approximately a quarter past three. Theologically, I can see that The Lord is all powerful and that we are small and insignificant. Meteorologically, I suspect that we will have, a beautiful day tomorrow. What does it tell you?"

Holmes was silent for a minute, and then spoke. "Watson, you idiot, it tells me that someone has stolen our tent!"

Sometimes that's the way it is with a prophetic person. They think in symbols and pictures. They read all manner of things into each and every situation, and they miss the most practical application of what they're looking at.

For example, a prophetic individual is driving down the freeway and realizes he is going the wrong way. Since he just passed exit seven he thinks to himself, "Seven is the perfect number so I must be in the perfect will of God." He turns around at exit eight, and since eight is the number of new beginnings, he thinks to himself, "The Lord allows us to make mistakes and start anew. Even though I made a mistake I am in the perfect will of the Lord."

The truth is, this prophetic person probably just missed his exit—plain and simple! I am not trying to make fun of the prophetic here, but sometimes we try to spiritualize something that is not very spiritual at all. It is just a human error.

If prophets make these kind of statements too often, it turns people off. When prophets do speak the true word of the Lord, people may question them because they think they are coming from another world again.

The truth remains, however, that someone with a prophetic gift goes through life looking at everything and anything through a prophetic lens. This is just how they view life.

My friend Calvin is a prophet who often receives direction from the Lord in seemingly unconventional ways. It will often go something like this. He is awakened in the early morning and glances at the digital alarm clock. It reads 4:22. Immediately he senses that the Lord wants him to travel to a neighboring town because 422 is a route number that runs through that town. He falls back to sleep and is awakened again at 5:01. He knows instinctively that he is to travel to one of our churches in this town because routes 501 and 422 intersect at that location. The Lord has been doing things like this in a consistent manner in Calvin's life. It is just the way the Lord has chosen to work in his life. And when he listens and responds to these promptings, people are blessed.

Time-tested maturity

As with the apostolic, the prophetic is a time-tested ministry. It requires a time of maturing and proving. We should be hesitant to place a title of prophet or prophetess on anyone before the proper amount of time passes through which they can be tested and matured. With the prophetic gift, this is especially critical because when the words "thus says God" are used, it carries tremendous authority and weight. How can you argue against what God says? We encourage young unproven prophets to instead use terms like, "This is what I sense the Lord is saying.," or "This is what I'm feeling." Or better yet, form a question, "Could the Lord be saying ...?"

There are two ways to bring the prophetic gift to maturity. It can either be matured and then released, or released and then mentored into maturity. One or the other is neither right nor wrong; it is just coming from a different perspective. It depends on how much a seasoned fivefold minister is willing to mentor a person as he or she functions in his or her gift.

My heart has always been to release the gifts, so I often encourage an individual to exercise his or her gift with the intention of mentoring the gift to bring it to maturity. Consequently, if a developing prophet speaks a word in a public gathering that is incorrect, they know that I love them enough to bring adjustment or correction to it in a loving manner. The Bible says we hear in part and prophesy in part. That means that we do make mistakes! We are not always 100 percent accurate. By mentoring the individual, I can help bring the prophetic gift into maturity.

The other way is to mature the gift and then release it. This is done through mentoring, training and teaching. As individuals continue to grow in their gifts, and I become more confident in their ability to hear the word of the Lord, I release them to speak at public gatherings. The goal is always to bring the prophetic gift to a place of maturity so that it will be a builder of the body of Christ.

Where can the prophet start to prophesy?

Many people do not know where to start in the prophetic ministry. I encourage individuals with a prophetic gift to start in a small group of people within a small group or house church where they can find a safe place to begin to exercise their gift. The person will make mistakes; that is for sure. The key is that they remain teachable and approachable as they continue to grow and mature. Over time, they will learn to hear the voice of the Lord more accurately and become more effective in ministering.

It is comforting to remember that all prophets started at this level at one time. It is also very helpful if someone more advanced in the prophetic is willing to be a spiritual parent mentoring the young prophet in this gift. Our family of churches offers one and two day Prophetic Training Seminars that are quite helpful in learning how to activate the prophetic gift in individuals. (For more information on attending or hosting such a seminar go to www.dcfi.org.)

The qualifications of a prophet

The qualifications of a prophet are the same as those of others in leadership.[4] Character is the main concern. As with the apostolic, a godly character is critical because prophets are the representatives of Christ. Revelation 19:10 tells us that the spirit of prophecy is the testimony of Jesus. Therefore a true prophet will speak forth the Lord's words with the Lord's heart.

The ministry of the prophet

They have an anointing to minister the Word of God. Lives will be changed when prophets minister God's Word in small groups and in local churches.[5] Prophets must know the Word of God so that no prophetic word will be spoken that is contrary to the Bible. The prophetic gift is a proclaiming gift: a prophet proclaims the word of the Lord. They are called to edify the body of Christ through the teaching and preaching of the Word of God.

They help mature and perfect the saints. Prophets desire to bring attention to areas of weakness in the body of Christ and minister until they see a strengthening in those areas. A prophet sees in his spirit weaknesses that must be addressed whether they are in individuals or the larger body. Theirs is a strengthening ministry, bringing the body to perfection, training them to fight for all that is rightfully theirs, giving no ground to the demonic. They desire to see the captives free and people restored to wellness.

They guide and release believers into their own ministries. Often a prophet will be used to either confirm a known gift in an individual or identify a gift "in waiting." They speak it as they see it, calling forth things that are either dormant or have been held back or through unfortunate life experiences have been intentionally shut down. A prophet brings possibilities back to life. It was Ezekiel who prophesied to the dry bones: "live." And they came to life! Prophets have that ability to identify ministries in others and want to release them into those ministries.

They carry an anointing for signs and wonders. A prophet will often minister prophetically through visions, dreams and prophetic utterances.[6] Prophets are in tune to the Holy Spirit. They will very often give words of knowledge to bring about healing to an individual or expose a problem in a congregation.

They confirm and/or give direction from the Lord. Prophets help give direction for individuals, small groups, local churches, families of churches, churches in a given community, or businesses in the marketplace. New direction from the Lord will be confirmed by the leadership responsible for those particular individuals or groups.[7] Prophets have their spiritual antenna up to hear from the Lord. They listen to what the Lord is saying and then speak it forth.

Prophets often deliver a prophetic word that will minister by exhortation (to stir up), edification (to build up), comfort (to strengthen), or conviction (to correct). Paul declared this in 1 Corinthians 14:3, "But everyone who prophesies speaks to men for their strengthening, encouragement and comfort."

Three aspects of a prophetic word

When receiving prophetic words it is important to understand that there are three aspects to every prophetic word. If we do not understand these three aspects, we are almost guaranteed a problem with the word.

Revelation The word is given out of the revelation of the Holy Spirit. I believe that many times the Holy Spirit will speak to us in words and pictures that we understand but that does not necessarily mean that we should share everything that we see in its entirety. The Lord may show me a drastic picture to drive home the importance of what He is saying, but I may share it in other terms or pictures to get the point across to the individual to whom I am ministering. I have seen people confused, not helped, by some words that were given exactly as they were received without using the discernment of the Holy Spirit to bring proper communication of the revelation.

Interpretation I heard one mature prophet say that people often hear what they want to hear. On one particular occasion, he had prophesied over someone who took what he said and tweaked it ever so slightly. With this new interpretation, the individual now had a "word of the Lord" to do what he wanted to do, but he had earlier been counseled by his local leadership not to do it! That is why every prophetic word needs to be discerned properly so that its true interpretation is heard.

Every prophetic word an individual receives should be shared with those to whom he is accountable because they have his best interests in mind. In the example that I just referred to, the individual went against the counsel of those who were praying for him because he had the "evidence" (the prophetic word) that he needed. Subsequently, he encountered much pain and heartache that could have been avoided had he been willing to follow the multitude of counsel of those around him rather than what he wanted to hear in the prophetic word.

Application Every word, when it is revealed and interpreted, needs to be applied. I like the example that my spiritual father, Larry Kreider, uses. "If the Lord shows me that my wife LaVerne has become an idol in my life, I don't get rid of her by divorcing her. No, I make adjustments and bring her to the right place in my life." The right revelation from the Lord (she has become an idol), with the right interpretation (she is lifted above Christ) but with the wrong application (I need to divorce her) will bring about pain and sorrow. It is all in the application. The right application (Jesus needs to be exalted above your wife) will bring about health and maturity in his life.

We need to have Spirit-led revelation from the throne room of God; we need to have accurate interpretation as to the meaning of the word; and we also need Spirit-led application so that the revelation and interpretation are carried out in a redemptive, kingdom-building manner.

Many times prophetic words that are given are conditional. If we follow through on our part, God will follow through on His part. God spoke over David that if he and his sons obeyed His commandments, the house of David would always reign over Israel. It was conditional upon their obedience. Of course we know that they didn't follow through on their obedience, and the kingdom was torn from David's descendants.

There may also be time frames to prophetic words. Some may be long, some very short. Take for example the story of Hezekiah recorded in 2 Kings 20 and also in Isaiah 38. The Lord told Isaiah to tell Hezekiah that he would die and not live. The Bible says in 2 Kings 20 that Hezekiah wept bitterly after Isaiah left. Before Isaiah got to the middle court of the king's house, the Lord spoke to him again and said, "Return to Hezekiah and say to him, 'I have seen your tears. I have heard your prayer, and I will heal you.'" In this case, the first prophetic word was only accurate for a very short time frame—until Isaiah reached mid-court of the king's house!

Then there was a new prophetic word given that was directly opposite of the first one. That's because God saw in Hezekiah's heart something that caused Him to make an adjustment to the previous prophecy—to add fifteen years to Hezekiah's life.

Prophets are not infallible in their ministry

Prophets hear in part and prophesy in part.[8] This means it is quite important for an individual receiving a prophecy to sense the affirmation of the Holy Spirit for that word in their lives. All believers are in a position to hear from the Lord for themselves. If that affirmation isn't there, the individual may need to lay the prophecy aside for awhile. I recommend reading Dr. Bill Hamon's short, easy-to-read book, *Fulfilling Your Personal Prophecy,* for more on this subject.

What is a false prophet?

Many people wrongfully think that if someone prophesies something that doesn't come true, he should immediately be labeled "false prophet." Since we all prophesy "in part," just because a prophetic word has some inaccuracy in it *does not* mean that the individual is a false prophet. A false prophet is someone who knowingly or unknowingly (if they are blinded by the enemy) tries to lead someone astray. False prophets will tend to bring division in churches and leadership and hinder the building of the church.[9] They are false in their character even if their words are true.

This is not to say that prophets should not be held accountable for their prophetic words. They do need to be held accountable, and when they deliver public words that turn out to be wrong, they need to publicly acknowledge their mistake. Personally I feel that this does not happen enough. Part of the character of the prophet needs to be one of integrity. If he speaks a prophetic word that is incorrect or only partially correct, then he needs to own up to it.

Prophets need a place to share the things they are seeing and hearing

A leadership team must provide a safe place for prophets to speak to the team. Whether this is a regularly appointed time or on an "as needed" basis, it is important that they have a place to "download" what they are hearing from the Lord. Otherwise, they will speak in the wrong place at the wrong time out of frustration, and there will usually be a mess to clean up! The words that are brought forth also need to be responded to properly. One of the most destructive things a church leadership team can do to a prophet is not to respond to a word the prophet gives. The prophet is left in the dark not knowing if the word was accurate, all wrong or just ignored. Leadership must decide if it is from God or not or if the timing is wrong. A prophet must learn to be the delivery person of the word and let it go. He cannot take it personally if it is not accepted immediately or acted upon. In other words, a prophet cannot "own" the word.

"Owning" happens when the prophet begins to feel a personal responsibility to see the word acted upon. He gets very frustrated if the leaders do not do what he prophesied. At this point, he has just crossed the line. A prophet is meant to deliver the word to the correct receiver. It is up to those who are responsible for the church where the word was given to apply and implement it.

Be careful about specifics

I tell all of the prophetic people in our family of churches to be extremely careful in prophesying about two things: prophesying dates and prophesying relationships.

Many people have been defrauded, hurt, disappointed and disillusioned by individuals who have prophesied specifics in these two areas. There is nothing wrong for a prophet to say that he feels there is something significant about a time frame, but the wording should be very generic. The same goes for prophesying about marriage relationships. Allow the Lord to bring two individuals together.

Certainly, we all know of positive stories where God spoke prophetically concerning two people coming together in a marriage relationship. It does happen. By contrast, there are far too many cases where two people got married based on a prophetic word, and there are all kinds of problems later. I believe when we become "Holy Spirit Matchmakers" we are on dangerous ground.

I remember one young prophet coming to me confused over whether he should marry a particular young woman. Another prophet had prophesied that he should marry her and yet another had said not to. "I don't know what to do," he lamented. "I honor the prophetic, and I don't know who to believe."

My counsel to him was that he did not need a prophet to speak into this situation; he needed a pastor who could care for him and give him insight so that he could hear from the Lord for himself. He should marry someone he loves and to whom he could make a lifetime commitment. Both should know God's personal affirmation on whether or not to get married. With well-rounded counsel, he could make a solid decision concerning the monumental decision with whom he would spend the rest of his natural life. He received that counsel and chose to marry. Today the couple has a solid family and is a vital part of the local church in their community.

The difference between prophesy and discernment

A discerning individual may look at a situation and discern what is wrong. But a prophet will look at the situation and prophesy correction or a solution to bring life to the situation. Take for example the dry bones that Elijah saw. Anyone with discernment could see that the bones were dry, but a true prophet will speak life to the brittle bones. A true prophet speaks the word of the Lord to a situation that brings "life" to it.

Someone with discernment only sees the problem, whereas someone with a prophetic gift sees the problem and prophesies the solution. That is a gift of prophecy at work.

The Lord always has a solution to a problem. Let's not take the prophetic gift for granted as we strive for accuracy in the prophetic words God gives. The prophetic gift remains an extremely important and much needed gift in the body of Christ. Jesus has given us this ministry gift so we can become more mature and hear what He is speaking to the church today.

CHAPTER 8

Evangelists Gather

Probably the best-known evangelist of our time has been the Rev. Billy Graham. As a child, I remember watching him on TV, listening to him preach a simple gospel message, hearing George Beverly Shea sing the special musical number, and then watching in amazement as thousands of people streamed out of their seats in the stadium and headed toward the platform. How did he do that? Were his sermons that well prepared? Was it the singing of George Beverly Shea? Were they offering free gifts down front?

No, there were no gimmicks involved. Granted, there were usually many churches in one city working together to sustain a successful crusade, but one of the main reasons for such a huge response was the fivefold anointing of evangelist Billy Graham. That anointing brought thousands of people in every crusade to the understanding that they needed to get in a right relationship with God as they asked Jesus into their hearts. Such is the anointing on evangelists. They have a passion for souls, and the fire in them is contagious!

The evangelist

The evangelist is another aspect of who Jesus is. He is the evangelist of evangelists. There was no greater evangelist than Jesus.

Jesus preached of Himself to a dying world:

> I am the way and the truth and the life. No one comes to
> the Father except through me.[1]

Evangelism means *to announce the Good News*. What is the Good News? Jesus has come. That is what He was proclaiming during His time here on earth. Jesus Christ has come and paid the price for your sin. Jesus Christ is the evangelist and His ministry on earth was to spread the Good News that He had come to save mankind.

Gift of evangelism desperately needed in the church

The gift of evangelism is deeply needed in the western church. Statistics tell us that most of the western world church growth is really "transfer growth" rather than "conversion growth." In other words, people are just moving from one church to another—most often from smaller churches to larger churches.[2]

Our hearts should cry out, "Where are the evangelists?" "Why isn't the church having more new births in Christ?" Jesus said that He gave "some with the gift of evangelism," and it is their responsibility to train and equip the rest of the body, releasing them to do the work of ministry. Herein lies much of the problem in the western church—training.

So often, we think that the person with the gift of evangelism is the one who should lead people to Jesus and the rest of us are off the hook. We erroneously think, "If only we had more Billy Grahams to do the work and then the world would get saved." That is a misunderstanding of Ephesians 4:12-13.

From this scripture, it is clear that evangelists are called to be training and equipping while they are doing ministry. They must train others in order to "prepare God's people for works of service, so that the body of Christ may be built up until we all reach unity in the faith and in the knowledge of the Son of God and become mature, attaining to the whole measure of the fullness of Christ."

Part of "the fullness of Christ" is that every believer would have a heart for the lost—those who do not know Christ. Hence the evangelist comes on the scene to stir our hearts to share our faith in Christ. Acts 1:8 says, "You shall receive power when the Holy Spirit comes upon you and you shall be my witnesses...." Evangelists stir our hearts to seek the Holy Spirit for more power to be His witnesses.

The difference between the gift of evangelism and a fivefold evangelist

Obviously not all are called to the fivefold ministry of evangelist spoken of in Ephesians 4:11. In fact, most of us are not. Nevertheless, we are all called to minister with our gifts. "As each one has received a gift, minister it to one another, as good stewards of the manifold grace of God."[3]

As with each of the other five gifts listed in Ephesians 4, to be a fivefold evangelist you need to have five aspects working in your ministry.

1. You have a discernible and operative gift.

2. You have the ability to identify that gift in others.

3. You have the ability to activate that gift in the individual.

4. You have the heart to nurture the gift in an individual's life to help bring it to maturity.

5. You have the ability to release others into ministry.

The calling of an evangelist

Fivefold evangelists are carriers of tidings. They carry a passion and desire to see people saved. They have a call of the Lord that has supernaturally equipped them with the ability to lead others to Christ. Alan, an adviser to our family of churches, teaches from Matthew 4:23 that Jesus came to preach the gospel of the kingdom and to demonstrate the power of the kingdom. That is the heart of an evangelist—to preach the gospel of that kingdom, drawing unbelievers to the saving knowledge of Jesus and demonstrating the power of the kingdom. The demonstration of that power sets free those who are oppressed by the devil. They also have a desire to train other believers to effectively reach the lost for Christ just as Jesus, the evangelist, trained His twelve disciples to reach the lost of His day.[4]

The qualifications of an evangelist

The qualifications of an evangelist are the same as that of any other fivefold minister. They must be of sound character and persons of integrity. They are to be full of the Holy Spirit and power. Philip, the evangelist,[5] was full of the Holy Spirit.[6]

Evangelists must be sound in doctrine since a large part of their ministry is preaching the Word.[7] A fivefold evangelist knows how to preach with authority and power. Many times an evangelist is not one who has lots of notes and points in his message. He simply opens his mouth and preaches Christ. Unlike the teacher who spends hours putting a sermon together with notes and point after point, an evangelist studies but often speaks more from the well within vs. a prepared text. He normally will have a clear sense of where he is headed in his preaching, but it is not laid out as plainly as a teacher's message would be.

Some people struggle with this concept. One evangelist told me, "My wife thinks I never prepare for a message, and I wonder if I am doing something wrong. It is very hard for me to come up with an outline for my messages. It is hard for me to preach off of notes like that."

I assured him that he is okay, and instead of preparing specific line-upon-line notes for his messages, he needs to study to keep his well full so that as he teaches and preaches, he is drawing from a deep well that has revelation from previous weeks of spending time with the Lord.

I find that many evangelists function this way. It is part of the nature of how their gift operates. This is part and parcel of their ability to start anywhere and preach Christ.

The affirmation of an evangelist

As with any of the fivefold gifts, a fivefold evangelist must first be affirmed by the leadership team in his local church and serve his local church in modeling evangelism as a life-style. After he has proven himself there, he may be released to the next level of ministry, as was mentioned in Chapter 4.

One of the different aspects of the evangelist is that the Lord will affirm evangelists by signs and wonders that follow them. These signs and wonders are for setting captives free and for drawing people to Christ.[8]

Individuals with a strong emphasis on signs and wonders are often called *power evangelists*. Signs and wonders are meant to be a tangible expression affirming that God is present desiring to minister to people. When Jesus laid hands on the sick, He often said, "The kingdom of God is near you." Signs and wonders bring us to the place where our hearts are separated from reasoning and free to respond to His Lordship because we cannot deny His power at work.

Evangelists with signs and wonders following their ministries need strong moral fiber and character so they do not misuse their anointing. Otherwise they would not be able to fight the temptation of accepting exorbitant favors, gifts and finances from people served by their ministry. Misusing their anointing can taint them as they get caught in the trappings of ministry instead of purely doing the Lord's work.

We cannot use ministry for selfish gains. According to 1 Timothy 6:6, "... godliness with contentment is great gain." My wise friend Billy once said, "When you start longing for material things they begin to possess you."

When you are striving for possessions, you will be tempted to use ministry as a means to get them. If you are an evangelist and move in the power gifts, the temptation will be greater because the opportunities will be more frequent.

One time, in Taiwan, as I was ministering prophetically over people, a young woman was next in line. The Lord ministered to her in a powerful way and at the end, she reached up and took off her two diamond earrings and placed them in my hands. I didn't quite understand, so I turned to my interpreter, "What shall I do?"

"It is up to you," he said, "she wants to give them to you for your wife as a gift for coming here."

My mind thought, "They look very valuable," but my spirit said, "Something isn't quite right here." I listened to my spirit. I told the interpreter to thank her but I placed the earrings back in her hands and told her to keep them until tomorrow and she should ask the Lord again whether He wanted her to give them to me.

I finished ministering and went back to my hotel for the evening and asked the Lord about it. He told me that because of her Buddhist background, she was accustomed to bringing a gift for the gods. Because I was now representing God by ministering there, she was carrying over a custom that was part of her life for many years. I shared this with my interpreter and she affirmed what I was saying. She also thanked me for not accepting the earrings the night before.

That evening, there was again time for ministry, and this woman again showed up in line. This time, I could see the embarrassment on her face as she apologized for wanting to give me her earrings. She had also prayed the night before and the Lord showed her that she was carrying over an old custom that was not of God. Had I not had the integrity of the Lord, I would have blindly accepted this expensive gift which was not meant for me.

The ministry of an evangelist

A large part of the ministry of the evangelist is to the unsaved. Their passion is to bring people to Christ. D.L. Moody once prayed, "Lord, give me the ability to lead someone to You every day for the rest of my life." One night he was crawling into bed and realized that he had not led anyone to the Lord that day. He immediately got out of bed went out into the street, found someone and led that person to Jesus. That is a pure evangelist.

Fivefold evangelists have a supernatural ability of knowing where an individual stands spiritually, and starting from that point, they begin to preach Jesus to him or her.[9] I love this about an evangelist. They can start anywhere, talking about anything, and end up talking to the individual about Christ. A friend of mine, Roger, is a great example of an evangelist. I was with him one time standing at a bus stop in New Orleans. A man came walking up to the bus stop in nice cowboy boots and a cowboy hat with a long beautiful feather sticking out of it. Roger immediately walked over to the man and commented about his beautiful hat. Within a few minutes he was talking to that man about Jesus.

In Acts 8:35, an Ethiopian eunuch was reading from a passage in Isaiah and asked Philip to explain the scripture to him. Verse 35 says, "Then Philip opened his mouth, and beginning at this scripture preached Jesus to him." Philip is a prime example of an evangelist because he had the ability to start anywhere and preach Jesus.

Fivefold evangelists have a God-given supernatural ability to bring the conviction of Christ to people, both individually and in large crowds, to the point where they feel compelled to come to Christ.[10] After Philip finished sharing with the Ethiopian eunuch, the eunuch wanted to get saved immediately. "Here is water, what hinders me from being baptized?"

A teacher can teach for an hour on the need for people to give their hearts to Jesus, explaining the atonement and the resurrection of the Christ. He will ask for those who want to get saved, and there will be a measured response. But an evangelist can preach to the same crowd a much shorter message and say something like, "You need to get saved tonight." Quite often there is a large response and people will be eager to get saved. It is supernatural—not trained or learned. It is a gift from God. Its origin is Jesus, and it is meant to bring people to Christ.

Fivefold evangelists stir up the body of Christ to reach the lost. Their desire is to see others in the church receive a burden for evangelism. You can always tell the difference between an individual who has an evangelistic gift and one who is truly a fivefold evangelist. A fivefold evangelist ministers to you in a level of grace that encourages you. After his evangelistic message, you cannot wait until the meeting is over so you can go and share Jesus with someone. A fivefold evangelist releases a gift of faith into your heart that says, "I can do this!"

Conversely, someone with an evangelistic gift but who is not a fivefold evangelist may cause you to feel guilty that you are not reaching more people for Christ. False guilt is not a motivator, but if it is conviction from God it is a great motivator. A passion for the lost and faith that the Lord has given you the ability is a motivator that brings results. That is the job of the fivefold evangelist.

One of the best ways to practice evangelism is to start at the small group level. If your small group lacks an evangelistic fervor, invite a fivefold evangelist to come to your group to stir up God's people in evangelism and give practical training in reaching the lost. A fivefold evangelist will motivate people to come to a place of faith, excitement and anticipation of sharing Jesus with others.

A small group leader shared with me that his group lacked motivation for outreach to the lost. He invited one of our recognized fivefold ministers to come teach and breathe evangelistic fervor into his group. The evangelist trained the group in evangelism principles for two evenings. On the third gathering of the group he led them on a street evangelism exercise in his local community. Upon their return, the small group was alive with excitement and testimonies.

Fivefold evangelists disciple other evangelists so they can be released for the harvest. Fivefold evangelists want to see themselves multiplied. They're not only interested in bringing others to Christ, their desire is to train and release many more like-minded individuals. There was a fivefold evangelist in New Zealand who spent years discipling more than twenty young evangelists. He was multiplying himself. This is true spiritual parenting.

Fivefold evangelists are called alongside the other fivefold ministers to bring the body of Christ to a place of maturity and perfection.[11] They carry zeal and a holy fire that ignites the body of Christ drawing them into a life-style of ministry. Fivefold evangelists especially are co-workers and extensions of apostolic ministry.[11] They help to extend the frontiers of God's kingdom.

Each of the fivefold gifts carries a different personality. It is not always easy for fivefold ministers to relate to one another due to the strengths of their gifts and the fact that each views life from the strength of that particular gift. But it is a good thing that one of the dynamics of Jesus' presence in our lives is the ability to walk together in unity. There is room for all the gifts.

While the gift of the evangelist is one of the most widely recognized gifts to the body of Christ, it is as much needed today as ever. We need evangelists to impart zeal for souls to be saved and to equip the saints with wisdom and anointing in winning the lost.

So, how do you get started?

An evangelist starts by sharing Jesus with others. As he continues to see more and more people coming to a personal relationship with Jesus it becomes clear that there is a gift at work within him. He begins to share his experiences with the small group of which he is a part. They are energized and excited by his testimonies. Some of them invite their unsaved friends to their house while this young evangelist is there, and through the course of the evening see their unsaved friends led to the Lord. An evangelist continues to walk in submission to the local leadership making himself available to encourage others in sharing Jesus with their unsaved friends.

As time goes on, and he is found faithful, continuing to labor alongside of others within the small group and larger congregation, the leadership team may ask him to do some teaching on evangelism. He willingly agrees. Others are encouraged and motivated to share their faith. The young evangelist begins to see this budding gift in others and nurtures that gift in them, encouraging them to begin to use it more frequently. The leadership team, observing his faithfulness and effectiveness, ask him if he would be willing to serve as a fivefold minister of the local congregation.

Just like other fivefold ministries, an evangelist starts by faithfully using the gift the Lord gave him, not looking for a position or looking for a title, but only desiring to be used by the Lord to bring others to Christ.

CHAPTER 9

Pastors Guard

A story is told of a pastor and evangelist who were bear hunting in the mountains. The pastor awakens the first morning and isn't feeling very well, so he decides to stay behind in the cabin. This does not deter the evangelist, however, who enthusiastically treks out into the mountains to hunt a bear by himself. About two hours later, the pastor hears the evangelist yelling and screaming and running down the mountain toward the cabin with a big black bear in hot pursuit. "Open the door, open the door!" the evangelist yells. The pastor quickly opens the door to the cabin, and the evangelist charges through with the bear on his heels. The evangelist continues straight out the back door, slamming the door behind him as he yells, "Kill 'em and skin 'em, and I'll go get us another one!"

This humorous story reveals how it sometimes feels to be a pastor. The evangelist brings them in but doesn't want to get involved in the more difficult work of discipleship. The evangelist is off getting the next person saved, but the pastor wants to get the people cleaned up before too many new ones come in and he is overwhelmed.

I personally understand this divine tension because I pastored a church for twelve years. Although I am now giving apostolic oversight to churches within our network, I still remember the pressures of being a pastor of a local church. They were some of the most exciting times of my life but also some of the most difficult.

There is probably nothing more exciting for a pastor than to see someone growing in the Lord. I was a pastor, by name, for twelve years, but there were a number of years prior to that when I poured my life into people—in essence, I was doing the work of a pastor. Shortly after Bonnie and I were married, I remember sitting in a prayer meeting at the church we were attending and the subject of demons came up. After some discussion, one of the leaders of the church spoke up, "You are talking about something that we know very little about, and it would be best to leave it alone." I immediately remember thinking, "That's fine for you but what about the person who has the demon? Shouldn't we be trying to find out more so that we can help the individual who is demonized?"

Even before I knew what it was, my heart of a pastor was influencing the way I was thinking. So, years later, as I began to see that heart develop, I became involved in deliverance ministry and have seen many people set free over the years from demonic oppression and influence. I'll never forget my first experience. A young man who was involved in New Age practices called me to say that he was through with life and he was going to have an out-of-body-experience and never come back. I didn't know if that was possible, but I was assuming that he was planning to commit suicide. After talking with him for quite some time trying to convince him to come to my house and he refusing each time, I finally blurted out, "I command you in the name of Jesus to come over here." He said, "Okay, I'll be right over."

Now I was shaken! "What do I do now?" I wondered. The Lord gave grace, and I have learned many things in the realm of deliverance ministry since then. A pastor loves to see people set free. He is their shepherd and when they are hurting, he is hurting.

I have spent nights driving around and stopping outside at people's houses to pray for them because I knew they were going through difficult times. I have fasted for them, prayed into the night for them, got up in the middle of the night standing in the gap for them, all without them or anyone else ever knowing. A pastor can easily do things like that because he sees the eternal value of people's lives.

There were times, when I was the owner of a large dairy farm, that I would get up every hour throughout the night to check on farm-related issues. I remember one night when the temperature was so cold that I needed to check the barns every hour to make sure that nothing froze. I always thought if I could awaken every hour, on the hour, for *cows*, I could certainly do it for *people*. People are eternal beings. It was always so exciting to me to see people delivered from addictions and other things that kept them from pursuing all that the Lord had for them. Such is the heart of a pastor.

Now when you give your heart to people like that you can be sure that you are opening your heart up to the possibility of being hurt. Some of the people that I have helped the most have been the ones who have hurt me the most. A pastor must guard his heart and minister to people "as unto the Lord" and not take it personally if they do not respond in the way he expects. One of the reasons a pastor can do this is found in 1 Peter 5:4, "And when the Chief Shepherd appears you will receive the crown of glory that will never fade away."

The pastor is not looking for the reward today; he knows that if he is faithful he will receive his full reward when the Chief Shepherd comes. In fact, he does not want his full reward today; he wants it when Jesus arrives.

Pastors run to the rescue

Years ago when I was still a small group leader, an international minister spoke at our church and shared from 1 Samuel 17:34-35. This story about a shepherd's motivation made a huge impression on me.

But David said to Saul, "Your servant has been keeping his father's sheep. When a lion or a bear came and carried off a sheep from the flock, I went after it, struck it and rescued the sheep from its mouth. When it turned on me, I seized it by its hair, struck it and killed it."

There are times when the enemy (lion or bear) has people caught in its deadly grip. The lamb is in pain and does not always know where that pain is coming from or how to get out of that deadly grip. It just knows that it is in pain and its only defense is to kick. In comes the shepherd (pastor). He runs to the rescue, praying and physically getting involved in the battle with the enemy. As the shepherd gets close to the bear to save the lamb, he will probably get kicked in the mouth by the lamb as it struggles for freedom. Sometimes the lamb can be so confused that it isn't sure who is trying to set it free or who the enemy is.

It can be likened to what happens when someone tries to save a drowning victim. The drowning person often struggles furiously, and they both can drown in the struggle. As the shepherd is in the process of attacking the bear, he sometimes becomes the bad guy. This can be difficult emotionally for the shepherd. All he is doing is trying to offer help and assistance. There have been many times that I have felt kicked in the mouth by the one caught by the bear.

I specifically remember one time after Bonnie and I had poured our lives out for a couple—helping them with their children, giving them groceries, giving our personal time and finances and also finances from the church—they came to a point where they didn't want anything to do with us anymore. One particular Sunday when we were dropping them off after church, they were angry with us because there was something they wanted us to do for them but we had other plans and could not help them. They told us, "You have never done anything to help us!" That was getting kicked in the mouth.

But wait, it gets worse. David says that after he delivered the lamb out of the bear's mouth, the same bear came after David. Pastors need to understand that sometimes they not only get kicked in the mouth by the "lamb," but after the lamb is set free, they get backlash from the enemy because they are successful in delivering the lamb from the enemy's grasp.

There are spiritual dynamics at work here that pastors must understand or they will walk away discouraged and disillusioned thinking that everyone is against them.

Charles Simpson wrote a book entitled, *The Challenge to Care,* one of the best books I have read on pastoring. He said, "Being a pastor is not an office. If you are looking for an office, go downtown and rent one. Being a pastor is a call from the Lord!"[1]

You must be sure that it is the Lord who has called you and not man, or you will not be able to withstand the pressures of ministry. If you do not have the Lord's calling, you will be a hireling. A hireling is a person who has no intention of staying or loving, but only holds his position as a convenient step toward bigger and better things. A hireling will run when the difficult times come because he does not have God's call to hold him in place.

When you lay your life down for the sheep and open your heart and life to their needs, you make yourself vulnerable like none of the other fivefold gifts. There is a potential for hurt and disappointment, but the opportunity for reward is also much greater because you open your heart and life in a way that can be very rewarding and fulfilling.

A pastor is a shepherd

Another name the Bible gives for a *pastor* is a *shepherd*. A shepherd has a compassionate heart. He listens to everyone's problems and cares about people because he wants them to be safe and protect them from harm. The shepherds of the church are to protect and guard the flock. It is their responsibility to provide protection, support, love and care. 1 Peter 5:1-4 gives an excellent job description for pastors.

> To the elders among you, I appeal as a fellow elder, a witness of Christ's sufferings and one who also will share in the glory to be revealed: Be shepherds of God's flock that is under your care, serving as overseers—not because you must, but because you are willing, as God wants you to be; not greedy for money, but eager to serve; not lording it over those entrusted to you, but being examples to the flock. And when the Chief Shepherd appears, you will receive the crown of glory that will never fade away.

There are several aspects to this fivefold gift as it relates to giving oversight to a body of believers.

1. Pastors shepherd God's flock as they give direction, protection and correction to it.
2. Pastors serve as overseers as they watch out for the people of God. They are guardians of the flock.
3. Pastors are willing servants not because they must but because they desire to be.
4. Pastors do not do it for the money or have hearts of greed.
5. Pastors do not lord it over people.
6. Pastors are examples that others will want to emulate.

The calling of a pastor

A pastor's calling comes from the Chief Shepherd. He is an under-shepherd serving under our Lord Jesus Christ. A true shepherd is not one who thinks, "I am going to try this pastor thing and see if I like it." It is a call from God. A pastor's calling is affirmed by the witness of the Holy Spirit in his own life and the fact that people are following him.

I remember one of our children having career day at their grade school. Someone asked if I wanted to come and share about my career as a pastor. The truth is, it isn't a career, it is a call. Pastors really should not look at their *calling* as a *career*.

In John 10:1-18, Jesus proceeds to state the character of a shepherd. In a parable, he shows the difference between a hireling and a shepherd and declares that He was the true shepherd and guide of His people.

"Most assuredly, I say to you, he who does not enter the sheepfold by the door, but climbs up some other way, the same is a thief and a robber. But he who enters by the door is the shepherd of the sheep. To him the doorkeeper opens, and the sheep hear his voice; and he calls his own sheep by name and leads them out. And when he brings out his own sheep, he goes before them; and the sheep follow him, for they know his voice. They will by no means follow a stranger, but will flee from him, for they do not know the voice of strangers." Jesus used this illustration, but they did not understand the things which He spoke to them. Then Jesus said to them again, "Most assuredly, I say to you, I am the door of the sheep. All who ever came before Me are thieves and robbers, but the sheep did not hear them. I am the door. If anyone enters by Me, he will be saved, and will go in and out and find pasture. The thief does not come except to steal, and to kill, and to destroy. I have come that they may have life, and that they may have it more abundantly. I am the good shepherd. The good shepherd gives His life for the sheep. But a hireling, he who is not the shepherd, one who does not own the sheep, sees the wolf coming and leaves the sheep and flees; and the wolf catches the sheep and scatters them. The hireling flees because he is a hireling and does not care about the sheep."

In this passage, Jesus states that He is "the door." He is the one who opens it for those who are called to be pastors. This calling must be "His call" placing individuals in this role of leadership. If an individual is not called by God, the person enters this role as a thief and a robber. This kind of individual does not care about the flock and is not a true shepherd. A true shepherd will not run when the trials come; instead he stays at his post and guards and protects the sheep that the Chief Shepherd has entrusted into his care.

A pastor nurtures those entrusted to his care

Jesus is the one who decides which sheep are entrusted into a particular shepherd's care. 1 Corinthians 12:18 says we are members of His body and He puts the members in place, deciding who goes where, and He does it as it pleases Him. I'll never forget something a man of God once told me. He said, "Don't complain about the people the Lord brings you. The Lord wants to use you in their lives, but sometimes He uses them to work something in your life as well."

This scripture frees us to understand that it is not up to a pastor to try to build a big church. Psalm 127 seems to reiterate this thought: "Unless the Lord builds the house, they labor in vain who build it"(NKJV). Unless the Lord is the One building the church, we are trying to get people to come that He hasn't ordained to come. Granted, we need to be about the Father's business of seeing the kingdom advance and people coming into the kingdom, but He is ultimately the one who causes that to happen.

As we trust God to give the increase, the church will grow. Everything that has the life of God in it grows. Everything that God created on earth that has life has the ability to multiply. The kingdom of God is no different. Every small group, every church, every network of churches should have a vision of multiplying. Anything less is just not God's best for them.

The exciting result is that as the flock goes about the Father's business of being a witness for Him, people will get saved. Whether or not they come to my church is up to Jesus, the Chief Shepherd. If He wants them to go to the church down the street that is okay by me; they are His sheep. My role is to care for those that He has entrusted into my care and advance the kingdom.

Pastors can act as God's mouthpiece to those they shepherd because they are there to exhort, comfort and uphold the believers in prayer. We receive spiritual protection, strength and oversight from the spiritual leaders the Lord places in our lives. As a spiritual leader, a pastor helps us to hear from God, often giving us words of advice. Obviously, the pastor must always allow us to make the final decision on hearing God's voice.[2]

Must the leader of a church be a fivefold pastor?

Often in today's church, the title of "pastor" is given to the one who leads a local church. This title then places certain expectations upon the role of pastor. The fact is that not every leader of a local church has the fivefold gift of "pastor." His primary gift may be that of an apostle, prophet, evangelist or teacher. If his primary gift is one of the other four gifts, it is very important that he has someone else on his team who has a strong pastoral gift to make sure that the flock is cared for properly.

If, for example, a church is led by an individual with the primary gift of an evangelist instead of a pastor, the church will mostly reflect a passion for the lost. Many people will get saved, but the evangelist, driven by the need to catch fish in the net, may neglect those already caught. This evangelist-led church may lose converts to another church that is led by an individual with the gift of pastor because pastors are those who look after, feed, protect and meet the needs of the sheep. That is why it is important that, if the primary gift of the individual leading a church is other than a fivefold pastor, he has someone who has a strong pastoral gift working alongside him.

Qualifications of a pastor

A pastor must have the heart of a shepherd, which means he cares deeply for the sheep. Character qualifications are the same as the other fivefold ministries which we will look at in Chapter 11.

Pastors have a God-given burden for the sheep. A hireling is in it for the remuneration and the role, but a true shepherd cares for the sheep even if there is not enough money to support him full-time. Because of his call to the sheep, he will look to the Lord to supply his financial needs another way. Many pastors are pastoring and ministering to people for years before anyone ever gives them the title of pastor.

I was operating a large dairy farm during the day and pastoring people at night for quite a few years before I carried the title. When I did receive the title of "pastor," it was an affirmation of something I was already doing. It didn't surprise or shock anyone because they had known my gift without the title. "That is who he is. We've seen it for years," many would comment.

Pastors are known by how they love and care for people. They carry God's heart and compassion for the sheep and will not run when adversity comes.[3] True shepherds do not scare very easily. They risk their lives and reputations for the sheep.

Characteristics of a pastor

Pastors have the God-given ability to assume long-term personal responsibility for the spiritual welfare of a group of believers. Receiving the personal care and accountability of a pastor helps believers feel secure and loved. Pastors keep, nurture and maintain the flock of God, leading them beside still waters and making them to lie down in green pastures. Those who give long-term direct oversight to small group leaders within the church must have a pastoral gift operating in their lives as well.

The pastors' authority is limited to those who have been entrusted into their care. We'll talk more about spiritual "fields" of ministry later, but it's important to understand that there are limits to the spiritual authority of pastors. A pastor's spiritual authority is limited to the individuals whom Jesus has entrusted to him. In a small group-based church, pastors spend much of their time equipping, training and serving small group leaders who, in turn, pour their lives into others.

The pastor trains and equips the body for ministry. The traditional pastor role in many churches dictates that he does most of the ministry. At least that is the mind-set of many people in the congregation. They believe that is why they support him.

There is a gravitational pull of ministry toward the front of an assembled congregation. Everyone who has ever ministered publicly has felt it. It leads to the misconception that the most valuable positions are center-stage positions. People begin to think that the only way to get proper ministry is to walk up front and receive special prayer from the person on stage. Nothing could be farther from the truth.

Keith, an adviser to our family of churches, has said that out of the forty power encounters that took place in the book of Acts, only one of them took place in the temple. The rest took place in the marketplace. Did you hear that? All but one of the miracles took place out on the streets, in homes and with the people. But in the Western world, we think that there must be a full worship band playing, with ministry only taking place at the front of the auditorium. I am not making light of the anointing and dynamics of that venue, but there does need to be a conscious effort by pastors as well as the other fivefold ministers to continue to not only equip the saints for ministry but to gently nudge and encourage ministry into the hands of the people. Go against the gravitational pull!

The early apostles didn't have time to do all the work. They were too busy praying and studying the word (Acts 6:3). The people were expected to be doing the ministry. When believers within a congregation understand that they are the ones who can minister, the congregation begins to grow. Believers will realize they have an important part to play and consequently will take ownership to it. Without that understanding they are looking to the pastor to make it happen.

Pastors of congregations are in place to see that training and equipping takes place regularly. They do not have to do all the training and equipping themselves. For example, if the group isn't growing, they can bring in a prophet and allow the prophet to blow out the cobwebs that have stifled growth. If the congregation does not have a vision for multiplication, a fivefold apostolic gift can be called in to stir things up by bringing attention to the greater purposes of God, rattling the cages of complacency and opening people's eyes to the surrounding world.

Apostles have the ability to stir the passion of Jesus in our hearts and spirits in such a way as to cause our flesh to get out of its comfortable mode of complacency and move into the exhilarating mode of action! Christ gave us the fivefold to train and equip His body so that we would not be anemic, tossed to and fro, but firmly grounded, steadfast, fulfilling the Lord's purposes for our generation.

A true fivefold pastor carries a father's heart and, therefore, has a desire to see people released in their spiritual gifts. He believes in everybody because he has seen where they have come from. During my pastoral days, sometimes an individual came to me with a concern about another person in the church. I often deflected their concerns by saying, "Joe is at the best place he has ever been. You don't know all that he has been through. We must be patient and love him."

Pastors take into consideration where people have come from and encourage them to go higher and farther in God. "You can do it!" is their battle cry. "The Lord is bigger than your problem."

The late John Osteen said one time, "Never say to God, 'Look how big my mountain is,' say to the mountain, 'Look how big my God is.'" I embrace that statement. Every pastor should portray that kind of attitude to the people. Sooner or later every person needs to decide whether they are a product of the things they have experienced in the past or whether they are a product of what Christ did on the cross.

True pastors are not threatened by others who have the same spiritual gift (or a greater measure of grace). Instead, as spiritual fathers they have a genuine desire to witness the body of Christ becoming mature. They desire others to go far beyond them in experience and anointing. They think in terms of "How can I see this individual grow and excel in the Lord? What does this body need to move forward in God? What can be done to see more people involved in ministry?"

A pastor carries the genuine God-given desire to bring healing to the flock. Psalm 23 gives a clear picture of the role of a shepherd in the church. At the end of the day a shepherd would always be looking over the flock. He carried a horn of oil to pour on the wounds of the sheep. A pastor has a heart to see people healed. He will incorporate various forms of ministry to see that happen—whatever form is effective for his group. His desire and heart's cry is to see people be all that they can be in Christ and for them to reach their full potential in God.

A pastor will not rule by lording over others but in humility lift the people before the Lord. A pastor must have the heart of a servant. Jesus is by nature a servant, and He looks for those with a servant's heart to be put in a place of service. The pastoral gift in Paul comes out in 1 Thessalonians 2:6-12:

> Nor did we seek glory from men, either from you or from others, when we might have made demands as apostles of Christ. But we were gentle among you, just as a nursing mother cherishes her own children. So, affectionately long-ing for you, we were well pleased to impart to you not only the gospel of God, but also our own lives, because you had become dear to us. For you remember, brethren, our labor and toil; for laboring night and day, that we might not be a burden to any of you, we preached to you the gospel of God. You are witnesses, and God also, how devoutly and

justly and blamelessly we behaved ourselves among you who
believe; as you know how we exhorted, and comforted, and
charged every one of you, as a father does his own children,
that you would walk worthy of God who calls you into His
own kingdom and glory (NKJV).

Notice the parenting language that Paul uses here. He behaved as a
father to those whom the Lord entrusted into his care.

A pastor has three basics needs in ministry

For a pastor to be effective in the on-going development of the
kingdom, he should have these three basic needs met and these gifts
functioning alongside him in ministry.

1. A pastor needs **insight**—a teaching gift helping him.
Since his primary gift is to care for people, he emanates love,
comfort and security. However, he needs the added insight
a teacher brings to his ministry so that people are firmly
grounded in the word of the Lord. A teacher's insight into
the weaker areas of the group will help to give direction to
the type and amount of teaching that is needed, focusing
on the weaker areas so they can be turned into strengths.

2. A pastor needs **foresight**—otherwise he will get caught
up in taking care of the needs of the people and forget the
direction in which he should be going. He needs a prophetic
voice speaking into his life and into the lives of the others
on the leadership team.

3. A pastor needs **oversight**—He needs someone with an
apostolic gift who can see the bigger picture. This person is
available to assist through difficulties and speak encouragement in the midst of trials. Many pastors have given up in
difficult times because there was no one there to encourage
them and help them see what was taking place in the larger
scope of things. An apostle can give hope and courage

and stir faith in the heart of the pastor while giving wise counsel and insight into body life. The pastor also needs the apostolic individual for vision for his flock and where his church is going. Too many pastors are "maintainers" and lack the ability to look ahead and chart the course. An apostle can help with this.

A pastor needs the teaching, prophetic, evangelistic and apostolic gifts speaking into his life and ministry so as to bring about God's full plan and purpose for His people. At times, this can be threatening to a pastor; however, when he sees that the others in the fivefold ministry are not trying to build their own ministries but helping to co-labor with him, he can trust them. The others in the fivefold are meant to come alongside and assist him in that purpose.

Is it possible to have a fivefold pastoral gift and not lead a congregation? Yes!

We said earlier that there is a difference between a fivefold ministry gift and the gift of government. For a fivefold pastor to lead a church, he must have a governmental gift.[4]

If he doesn't have the governmental gift to lead, he can still be a fivefold pastor. It would work this way: A fivefold pastor can be someone who carries all the ministry aspects of a pastoral gift but does not have the desire or anointing to lead a group of believers. He is an encourager, desires to see people healed, ministers healing to larger groups and trains others in healing. He may give oversight to small group leaders in the local church setting even though he is not on the leadership team. He is an excellent one to nurture other developing gifts, bringing them to maturity.

In a family of churches, he can sometimes give oversight to other pastors even though he would not be in a governmental position within that family of churches. He would be functioning with a mixture of an apostolic gift as well in this setting. He may not have a governmental role in the family of churches but he can certainly express his gift within boundaries given to him by the overseers of the movement.

Whether it is for five, five-hundred or five-thousand people, the Lord has given the awesome fivefold-pastor-gift to the body so that we do not become weak or wounded, weary or discouraged but instead whole and overcoming as the Lord intended us to be as the body of Christ.

CHAPTER 10

Teachers Ground

Twice a year we meet with the teachers of our children within our local school district. I'm always amazed when I meet with these wonderful schoolteachers. Year after year they teach similar information over and over again. Some of them have been teaching for more than twenty years. They have the God-given gift to be able to teach the same material from year to year while keeping it fresh and new. A math teacher's excitement comes from a whole new class of students catching the principle of an algebra problem and understanding how to solve it. A history teacher is thrilled when some of her students take an interest in World War II, desiring to understand all the world powers, lofty goals, plans and strategies, attacks and counterattacks that led up to the greatest conflict the world has ever known. A teacher's excitement stems from seeing someone else sharing his or her enthusiasm for a particular subject. I believe the same is true for fivefold teachers in the body of Christ.

Fivefold teachers ground believers in God's Word. They have the supernatural, God-given ability to teach the principles and doctrine of God in a life-giving way that can easily be understood and applied to everyday life. It is an anointing that imparts God's divine life to others. Their passion is to take something that is very difficult and teach it in a way that is easily understood and applied.

R. T. Kendall, an author and former pastor of Westminster Chapel in London, believes the church today desperately needs good teachers because "a dearth of solid teaching in the church reveals that the body of Christ needs more than good experience—it needs good theology." He goes on to say:

> The...teacher is the last on the list of...special anointings given in Ephesians 4:11. It is the least controversial, but possibly the most neglected and needed of the five. The Greek word for "teacher" (*didaskalos*) is found in the New Testament fifty-eight times. It was a common way the twelve addressed Jesus—"Master" in the King James Version—which appears in the four Gospels alone at least forty-five times.[1]

The calling of a fivefold teacher

A fivefold teacher is called by the Lord and affirmed by his spiritual leadership. He is filled with the Holy Spirit and power and is able to teach in a life-giving way that brings grace to those who hear him teach. Someone asked Spurgeon once, "What is the secret of great teaching?" He replied, "Get on fire with the gospel and people will come to watch you burn." This was the approach of the Psalmist in Psalm 39:3: "My heart grew hot within me, and as I meditated, the fire burned; then I spoke with my tongue."

The teacher is someone who ministers the word in such a way that releases God's power and anointing, encouraging believers to rise to their full potential in God. He has the ability to teach the Word of God accurately so that people are not fooled by false doctrine. He spends hours studying the word because his gift is to rightly divide the Word of Truth.[2]

A teacher's motto is "You shall know the truth, and the truth shall set you free."[3] His goal and passion is to conform us to the image of God while Christ is being formed in us.[4]

The Word of God is abounding with revelation, and while teachers love to teach foundational teachings, they also thrive to receive new revelation from the scripture. I've read the Bible through many times but I am still finding new things that I didn't see before. Such is the desire of a teacher, teaching foundations yet releasing revelations.

The qualifications of a teacher

The qualifications of a teacher are the same as with other fivefold gifts. Character is a qualifier.[5] Fivefold teachers must live what they teach, being an example to the body of Christ in word and sound doctrine. A teacher invalidates his ministry when his life does not line up with what he teaches. He becomes a "sounding brass or a clanging cymbal" and respect for him decreases. A teacher must live what he teaches, giving evidence to the Word of God at work in his life.

According to the Bible, a teacher will always be judged more strictly by the things that he teaches. I remember when this word from James 3 got my attention. The holy fear of the Lord caused me to realize that I had to be very careful when I stood before a group of people to teach.

Not many of you should presume to be teachers, my brothers, because you know that we who teach will be judged more strictly.[6]

I have noticed that some sort of life experience either tests or affirms the word I am preparing to teach. If I'm teaching on God's provision, very often that particular word will be tested in my own life. I come out of that testing with a firm understanding and reality of God's provision and I can give testimony to that fact the next time I teach on the subject.

If I'm teaching on marriage, undoubtedly I see this area challenged in my relationship with my wife, Bonnie. A teacher need not fear this God-scrutiny on his life. It really is an opportunity to prove the Word of God to be true. If what a teacher is teaching is not a reality in his life, then he should not be teaching it. It is always better to teach what we know to be true, what we have experienced, versus just a thought or concept. I appreciate a teacher that teaches *life*, not just *theory*.

A teacher has the ability to lead people astray or on the right path. That is a sobering thought. The average person will not take the time to study as much as a teacher does who publicly ministers. Therefore, there is a responsibility on the teacher's shoulders to make sure that what he teaches is truth and reality. He cannot say something just because it sounds good; it needs to be accurate, to line up with God's Word. A teacher stands in a place of spiritual authority and holds the destiny of the people that he is teaching in his hands. He wants to not only lay a good foundation but also build upon the foundation that has already been laid. A teacher is very conscious about confusion and strives to avoid it at all cost.

The "divine tension" of the fivefold gifts shows up with the teacher as well. Consider the tension between a teacher and a prophet in this scenario: A gathering of believers have come together for a time of worship and teaching. God's Spirit is present and there is tremendous freedom in worship. Prophetic words are given; people are drawn to the presence of God; there is excitement, anticipation, a sweetness in the spirit and an understanding that indeed the presence of the Lord is among them.

In this situation, the prophet will be thinking in terms of, "Let's just go a little longer; the presence of God is here; people are being changed by His presence; let's keep worshiping the Lord."

Meanwhile, the teacher is thinking, "Can we just get on with it? We have been worshiping for over half an hour; I won't have time to teach the full word; it's the implanted Word of God that will change their hearts; I wish I could have taught first, with the worship later." Can you not feel the divine tension?

The truth is that both are right. People are changed when they are brought into the presence of God. But the Word of God is also very powerful, sharper than any two-edged sword, able to separate soul from Spirit. So we need the presence of God in our lives *and* the power of God's Word as well.

The characteristics of a teacher

Teachers validate truth. A teacher has the need to validate truth, particularly doctrinal and theological truth. They spend large amounts of time studying and meditating on the Word of God. Spending time studying the Word is not a chore for them. They have inquiring minds and love to pour over scriptures to receive fresh revelation from the Spirit of God. Usually the more difficult task for a teacher is being able to take all that he knows and deliver it in a concise time frame so that others are able to receive it.

Teachers speak with authority. They know who gave them the words to speak; they are not teaching their own pet doctrines; they are teaching life from the very Originator of life, the Lord Jesus Christ. Teachers know these things to be true because they spent time in the presence of God studying and preparing, comparing scripture to scripture, verse to verse and translation to translation. They are confident that what they are teaching is true.[7]

Teachers have the ability to articulate and express thoughts. They have the God-given ability to take something difficult and make it amazingly simple and easy for people to understand. A teacher is not easily persuaded or tossed about by every "wind of doctrine."[8] They are like the Bereans (Acts 17) who searched the scriptures daily to determine whether the word was true or not. While we all should be like the Bereans, this clearly describes the fivefold teacher. He studies to show himself approved.

Teachers train and release. A fivefold teacher desires to train and release other teaching ministries.[9] They mentor future teachers. This kind of spiritual parenting simply means that older established teachers take others under their wings, pouring their lives into them so that they can become more effective in teaching the Word. Paul took Timothy under his wings, and as a spiritual parent, mentored Timothy by both biblical instruction and example.

There was a deep connection between the content of instruction and the example of the teacher, since the teacher would often be imitated by the pupil. One thus recalls Paul's final word to Timothy, "You, however, know all about my teaching, my way of life, my purpose, faith, patience, love, endurance" (2 Timothy 3:10). Doctrine and manner of life were intimately related.[10]

This was also exemplified by Aquila and Pricilla in Acts 18, when they saw a certain Jew named Apollos, who was a very eloquent man and mighty in scriptures, teaching in the synagogue. They took him aside and explained to him how to teach in a more accurate way concerning Jesus Christ. That is the spiritual fathering heart of a fivefold teacher.

Teachers desire to see many others released in teaching but hold fast to the preciseness of the Word and want the Word taught with accuracy. I can always tell when I am ministering and there is a teacher in the crowd. Sometimes I can tell by observing their body language that while I am teaching they are cross-referencing the verse that I have just read. Sometimes they come up to me afterwards for a more detailed explanation of what I just taught. Sometimes I am challenged by what I have spoken. This is the teaching gift in operation, and I appreciate it.

Again, there is a difference between someone who has a teaching gift and someone who is a fivefold teacher. Someone with a gift to teach has a discernible gift while someone who is a fivefold teacher has the other dynamics relating to a fivefold gift that we have already mentioned in Chapter 4.

Teachers possess a passion for God's Word. A teacher's passion is the Word, the Word, the Word. They carry a God-given desire to see the body of Christ reach a place of maturity so as to be able to handle the "meat" of the Word. They long for the deeper things of God and desire that the body of Christ hunger for it as well. They are builders in the kingdom, grounding believers in God's Word so they are firmly rooted and stand strong on the rock, Christ Jesus. Teachers build on a firm foundation and want others to do the same so that the body of Christ is immovable while under the attack of the enemy. They do not mind teaching the "milk" of the Word and can do it in a life-giving way, but they will become frustrated if people do not grow past the milk stage.

God matures His church through the fivefold ministry

The fivefold ministry is called by God to work together as a team. These gifts are not independent of each other but interdependent upon each other so that as they work together the body will be fully matured, grounded, taught, trained, equipped and released in ministry to reach a lost and dying generation who does not know God. Each ministry gift is needed. These gifts are not in competition with each other; they bring completion to the body. Each one carries certain aspects of Christ that are needed for His kingdom to advance. I am very excited that the Lord is restoring each of these gifts to His body because without them we will never fulfill His mandate. The church of our generation will only come to maturity in Christ as we receive from each of these gifts and as they walk together in unity.[11]

Fivefold Ministers Work With Local Church Leaders

God designed the church so we are interdependent on each other. Because the fivefold ministry gifts are so critically needed, it is important that church leaders endeavor to relate closely to these spiritual experts given to the church.

The role of workplace fivefold ministers

I want to mention here that fivefold ministers do not exist solely inside local church circles. These experts also exist in the workplace. When God calls people to minister for Him right where they are in their area of influence on their jobs, they can be functioning as fivefold ministers.

God does not have a secular business people and a spiritual church people. Whether we serve more frequently in business or in the local church, we must understand each other's ministry callings. There are many fivefold gifts at work in the marketplace, and often there is no place given for them to function in the local church. They flourish in the marketplace and the local church continues on without their gift or input.

With all the emphasis the last five years on marketplace ministry, the Lord is beginning to change that mindset. Peter Wagner believes God is releasing marketplace apostles and fivefold marketplace ministers around the world. He says, "I believe there are Apostles of Finance, Technology, Medicine, Industry, Education, the Military, Government, Law, Communications, Business, Transportation, Nuclear Science, Agriculture and a hundred other segments of society. When these Marketplace Apostles begin to move into their rightful place under the powerful anointing of God—watch out! Revival will be right around the corner!"[1]

While that is a separate topic, I agree with Peter Wagner that there are many fivefold gifts in use within the marketplace from which the church could benefit if local church leaders would open themselves up for their input.

Why fivefold ministers can be perceived as a threat

For too long, the translocal fivefold ministers have been looked upon as a threat to the one who leads a local church. The fivefold ministers have been accused of trying to build their own ministries rather than working with the local church. They have not been perceived as supporting the local church leaders to build in a way that would demonstrate unity. In some cases this is an accurate scenario. But there are reasons for this, which we will explore briefly along with looking at some guidelines to help the fivefold ministers and local church leadership work together in a way that God designed them to.

Fivefold ministers should regularly assist local church leaders

God gave the fivefold ministers so they could help build the church. They were meant to build alongside the local leadership and assist them in building the church. Because they often have not been properly cared for in the local church, many fivefold ministers shy away from the local church and tend to look after themselves. Subsequently, they have become more independent in nature and are sometimes viewed by others as being aloof, hard to work with and not willing to make an investment in their local church.

There are some sad stories of fivefold ministers who have come into a local church on a weekend, sown division, spoken out of place, and left on Monday morning with the senior pastor and his team left with a mess to clean up. Obviously, this does not further the cause of Christ and puts a bad taste in the mouth of a local leadership team for fivefold ministry. Therefore, they are sometimes held at arm's length by local church leaders, often viewed as ministers to be utilized for a short time and then sent on their way.

The truth is that fivefold ministers have been given by the Lord to assist leadership teams in building the church. God's plan is for translocal fivefold ministers to walk alongside leaders to help build the local church—not be used as "flash-in-the-pan" ministries and then leave again. I know that if I want to instill a heart for evangelism in people's lives, it isn't going to happen during one meeting. I can have a tremendous evangelist come into town, and we can have powerful meetings with many people responding to the altar call, but statistics prove that this kind of teaching is not very effective long-term. It would be better to have a fivefold evangelist come in on a regular basis several times a year to train and help turn people's hearts toward the lost and equip them to share their faith. In this way, the church is built systematically, step by step.

Fivefold ministers are called to build the church of Jesus Christ. They like to build systematically. They desire to build with a firm foundation and then systematically add to that foundation so there can be length, depth and breadth added to the local church. If a church leader has a fivefold minister come and minister only once every year or two, there is far too much time between installments for proper building to take place. Building systematically means the fivefold minister comes into a local congregation on a regular basis and builds on what was shared the last time he was there. This is, by far, many fivefold ministers' preference.

A new paradigm

The Lord wants to change our former way of thinking. The old paradigm involved giving the sole responsibility for feeding the flock to the senior leader of a church. All the teaching, training and ministry was to be completed by him on Sunday morning, Sunday evening, and Wednesday night.

The New Testament paradigm is for both the fivefold and local leadership to work together so they can bring the church to maturity and strength. To this end, the church is filled with the power of God with the saints doing the work of ministry as Jesus intended! I like what David Cannistraci says, "When we return to the pattern of the early church we will recover the power of the early church."[2] It cannot happen apart from fivefold ministers fulfilling their role in training, equipping and releasing the body of Christ.

The Lord wants to take us from a place where fivefold ministers and local church leaders function independently of each other and bring them to a place of interdependence, both realizing that they need each other. The translocal fivefold minister needs the local leadership team for accountability, affirmation of ministry and a place to see his gift used effectively. Local leadership teams need the fivefold ministry to work alongside them assisting them in training, equipping and releasing their local congregation into all that God has for them.

The worst mistake we can make at this point is to give up on the translocal fivefold ministers because of problems of the past. If we ignore these ministers, we lose their valuable contribution and impartation to the body of Christ. Jesus never intended the local leaders to work alone. He provided the fivefold ministry so that the pastor does not need to be "everything" the flock needs. Instead, he can draw from the anointing of the *evangelist* to see people saved and stir others with the desire to share Jesus with their friends and neighbors. He can receive the help of the *prophet* to keep the work on track and "up to speed." The pastor can draw on the *teacher* to impart the deeper things of the Word into people's hearts that is able to save their souls and bring about change. He can receive the help of the *apostle* to make sure they hold fast to the vision the Lord gave them and ensure a continuous outward and forward thrust of ministry. Not only can the pastor draw on these fivefold gifts, but these ministers impart into the lives of the people to bring them to a greater level of spiritual maturity. And, if the senior leader's primary gift is not that of pastor, he can draw from a fivefold pastor to assist in the work of caring for the needs of the people.

Local church leaders identify, train and equip fivefold ministers

It should be the goal of local church leaders to identify, train, equip and release fivefold ministers from within the local church. However, a local fellowship should not only desire to raise up fivefold ministers from within, they should invite fivefold ministers from outside of their local body to come in and minister. For example, if there is no fivefold prophet from within, a pastor should not wait until he has someone raised up; he should look to import a prophet from outside his church. He continues to bring the prophetic gift in until a prophetic gift is raised up from within. Over a period of time, the imported fivefold prophet is able to identify others of similar giftings within the local church body. He can be involved in training, equipping and releasing those individuals into the prophetic ministry.

Very often someone from the outside is able to give a fresh perspective on issues that could be overlooked by someone who is there among the people all the time. One of the abilities of fivefold ministers from outside the local body is their capacity to quickly identify others of similar gifts within a fellowship. These newly identified individuals and their developing gifts have the wonderful opportunity to learn from the "outside" fivefold ministers as they function together within that local fellowship. When fivefold ministers spend time with those who have a developing gift, they can impart much to them. The developing ministers can ask questions, talk about how their gifts should function and experience the anointing of an established minister. Another way of stirring the fivefold is to sow into other established fivefold ministries that you are lacking in your local church. For example, if we really need to see a prophet released, I will sow into an established prophetic ministry, believing that part of the increase is going to be establishing a prophetic ministry at that local church.

Accountability for a fivefold minister's personal life

Since accountability is such an important aspect of the Christian walk, it is important that clear lines of accountability are established for every fivefold minister.

Accountability for the individual's personal walk with the Lord and interpersonal relationships (both in his family and the local church) comes from his local pastor and leadership team. Every fivefold translocal minister needs to have a place that he calls home. Within a local body of believers—whether it is a house church, a larger church with small groups or a mega church—the fivefold minister needs to walk in submission to the local church vision as he lives in accountability with other believers within a local context.

Some translocal ministers say they are accountable to the relationships that they have established on the road as they minister on their travels. But let's be practical—there is a certain amount of accountability that happens when I see and talk to someone a few times a year, but in terms of practical accountability, I need to be connected on a local level. I should be in relationship with people who see me in my "everyday clothes."

It is easy to be enamored with the thought of traveling public ministry. When I minister in my travels, I use the best stories, talk about all the great things that are happening as I minister under "the anointing." By contrast, I need to have relationships that see me when my guard is down—when I just finished taking out the trash, the lawn mower broke and I don't have the message prepared yet for the weekend.

In short, I need to be walking and talking with people close to me in everyday life. Even if I am traveling to the nations, I need a local church expression with whom to walk in accountability. I am a part of a local church called "The Fireplace" and because of my traveling schedule, I miss many Sunday morning services. Nevertheless, when I am in town, I attend a small group and also a local gathering of small groups, which is The Fireplace. They know that I am submitted to them and a part of building the kingdom right there in my own community. I have a senior elder who will ask me how I am doing, who prays for me, and acknowledges my gift publicly, affirming the call of God on my life.

I help train small group leaders, take part in prayer meetings and even teach children's ministry on occasion. As much as possible, I am a vital part of the life flow of my local church.

Accountability for a fivefold individual's ministry

A fivefold individual ministers within a sphere **or** field **of ministry**. His sphere of ministry establishes to whom he is accountable (see page 129).

A fivefold individual ministers within a local church—from a small house church to a mega church—and receives accountability for his ministry from the leadership team of his local church.

A fivefold translocal individual ministers in a family of churches and receives accountability for his ministry from the apostolic leadership of that family of churches. Accountability for his personal life comes mostly from the leadership team of the local church he attends. In brief, there is some prayer support that comes from the apostolic leadership of the family of churches, but most of the practical accountability comes from those who walk with him in everyday life in his local church.

A fivefold translocal individual ministers to the body of Christ at large and also receives his accountability for his ministry from the apostolic leadership of the family of churches of which he is a part because that church family sent him out. There is some accountability as well from apostolic fathers in the church at large. Accountability for much of his personal life comes from the local church. But if there is a problem with his personal life and the local leaders are unable to deal with it, the apostolic leaders should be brought in to assist the local leadership.

What this means in relationship to his ministry is that if Joe Prophet prophesies something over Jane Christian that is clearly out of order, it is the responsibility of the leadership that released Joe to deal with the issue and bring correction. If Joe is a fivefold minister in the local church, the local leadership team walks through the correction and adjustment. If Joe was released by the apostolic leadership to the family of churches or to the larger body of Christ, then the apostolic leadership needs to bring adjustment and correction because it is outside the field of ministry of the local congregation.

See the gift released and mentor it to a place of maturity

The local church is the training ground for ministry. When I was a senior pastor of a congregation some years ago, I endeavored to allow people to use their gifts in the church as much as possible. This meant, however, that I had to be willing to mentor that gift. Sometimes this meant I had to bring correction when necessary, even in a public setting. For example, perhaps a prophetic word was given that was not clear. It was my responsibility as the spiritual leader of the church to clarify it and encourage the prophet to hear clearly the next time so the gift could be fine-tuned and brought to a place of maturity.

I often encouraged young teachers to try teaching in small groups first before giving them larger teaching venues. The small group is an excellent place to begin to develop any gift. I recommend fledgling teachers to take a simple "teacher training course" our church developed that helps to train teachers to teach the Word in a life-giving way (www.dcfi.org).

I learned to pastor in a small group. In fact, it was in a small group setting that I first realized that I had the gift of pastoring. As I was faithful in pouring my life into others, the leadership realized I had a God-given ability to give pastoral oversight to multiple small groups. As time went on, we planted a whole church from those small groups, and I became the pastor. It all started in a small group of people that my wife, Bonnie, and I loved and encouraged.

Norm is an church planter who recalls how effective it was to have a spiritual father, Chuck, who mentored him to a place of maturity in his gift.

> You can't be fathered by just joining an organization, sitting in meetings and having a few conversations on the phone. Chuck was a spiritual father who cared for my soul and spent time with me. God wanted me to voluntarily allow Chuck access into my life. Many are afraid to submit to another. They are afraid it may restrict them. I found it liberating. I had someone watching my borders. If I got off course, Chuck was there to sound the alarm. He didn't have his own agenda for my life, he simply had the heart of a true father. Although he taught some great messages, I mostly remember what I watched him do—how he dealt with people, situations and lived out his live in Christ.

You may ask, "What if someone has a gift and it is not noticed by the church leadership? Is it okay for that individual to approach church leadership and ask if he can be mentored in his gift? Of course! An individual should share what he senses about his gift and submit it to the local leadership for their discernment. They may say that more development or experience is needed, or ask that you attend a seminar or other time of impartation relating to your gift. As you submit your gift to that leadership, they will, in time, sense your heart of submission and trust will be built. When trust is built, you are well on your way to seeing your gift recognized. You can also show personal initiative by reading books on your gift, going to hear others who have a similar gift when the opportunity arises, in this way investing in the development of your gift.

A mantle is placed upon a fivefold minister

When I see a developing fivefold gift in an individual, my goal is to see him mentored and developed to a place where he can be released as a fivefold minister in the local church. When that happens, a mantle is placed upon him in the spirit to discern from the Lord the weak areas in that church body. If I, as part of the leadership team in the church, do not provide a place where he can give freely what the Lord has spoken to him, I will frustrate him.

That is the mistake I made as a senior pastor when I first encouraged the release of the fivefold ministry in our congregation. I had two prophets, one evangelist and one teacher whom I laid hands on in front of the congregation and commissioned them as fivefold ministers. I would give them an opportunity to speak several times a year. But they became frustrated, and I couldn't understand why. I thought I was giving them opportunities to speak what was on their hearts but the frustration remained. Then one day as I was reading through Ephesians, I realized what the problem was. I had given them a mantle (a responsibility) but I hadn't given them the key (the authority) to work it out.

To illustrate, let's say I tell you that you are in charge of keeping a certain room in the house warm but I don't show you where the thermostat is. When you do find it, it is under a glass case and locked. You would become frustrated because you could not adjust the heat even though I gave you that responsibility and you feel it is your God-given responsibility to fulfill. You might begin trying anything to keep the room warm. You might even build a fire in the corner, endangering the whole house!

When I understood that I was exasperating them by not giving them the keys to their ministries, I spent time with them discussing and praying about weak areas in our church body that we needed to strengthen. We would then decide together with the leadership team how it would be worked out. Immediately the frustration dissipated. They were no longer concerned if they were the ones to do the actual teaching and training, they just wanted to know that the things they were feeling were being heard and acted upon.

It is important to understand that the fivefold should speak into the leadership of the church and give them advice, but it is the leadership team's responsibility to make the final decisions as to how it will be carried out. Likewise, leadership teams need to listen and take advice from the fivefold ministers or things will come out the wrong way at the wrong place at the wrong time.

Fivefold ministers submit to those in authority

It is a fallacy for the fivefold minister to think that once he starts to move in the power and anointing of the Holy Spirit, he does not have to submit to the authority of the leaders of his local church. He may be tempted to think, "Well, my gift and anointing is greater than the leaders here, and I am above them."

Fivefold ministers should always be willing to be mentored by those who are placed in spiritual authority over them (Hebrews 13:17). When the Lord places individuals in a body, He does so for their protection and not to hold them back. There is tremendous freedom in that.

When I led a local church, I had men and women in the church who carried a greater anointing than I did. The ones who acknowledged my leadership continued to grow in anointing and influence. Sadly, the ones who felt they were above me did not grow as much in anointing or influence. It wasn't something I did. It was something the Lord was doing. We minister by our spirits, and the spirit of pride was emanating from those who felt they were above the local leadership team. With that type of mentality, it is almost impossible to receive instruction and correction. The Lord resists the proud but gives grace to the humble.

A good friend of mine, Duane, became part of our church before we ever recognized fivefold ministers. He had gone to seminary, planted a previous church and was much more gifted than I was. But he became a part of our congregation, submitting to me as a son would submit to his father. He served me and wanted to see me succeed. One of the first ways he served was by becoming an usher. I remember thinking, "This guy can preach rings around me, and here he is, simply ushering."

Recognizing his faithful service and anointing, I invited him to minister several times. He became a small group leader, then he and his wife and daughter went to Africa for two years as missionaries. Later, he pastored the largest church in the DOVE International family. He did it right. He came in with a heart to serve, walking in accountability, submitting himself to the vision that the Lord had for our local fellowship, and the Lord raised him up.

Fivefold ministers operate within a field of ministry

Paul encouraged the early Christians to boast only "within the limits of their sphere of ministry." These fields of ministry, assigned to us by God, are our spheres of influence, responsibility and anointing.

> For we dare not class ourselves or compare ourselves with those who commend themselves. But they, measuring themselves by themselves, and comparing themselves among themselves, are not wise. We, however, will not boast beyond measure, but within the limits of the sphere which God appointed us—a sphere which especially includes you (2 Corinthians 10:12-14 NKJV).

Paul understood his sphere of influence and reminded the Corinthians that he was only to operate in the sphere God had appointed to him. He only boasted of the Corinthian church because he was responsible before the Lord for them.

Coming from a farming background, this is an easy concept for me to grasp. When I was a farmer, I owned a two hundred acre farm. There were two other farms right beside mine, one of which

I rented from the owner. The other adjacent farm I neither owned nor rented. On my own farm, I could plant whatever I wanted, whenever I wanted. On the rented farm next door, I had delegated authority from the owner to plant certain things, but there were limitations. Of course on my other neighbor's farm, I had no authority whatsoever to plant.

Can you imagine what kind of trouble I would have had if I had decided, "Today's corn-planting is going so well; I have finished with my own fields, and there are still four hours of daylight. Since things are working so well here, I will go over to my neighbor's fields and continue to plant. No matter if he is planning to plant soybeans; I am sure he will understand my generosity and thank me for planting corn instead." Do you think he would thank me for this? I think not. It is not my field or my responsibility, and I have no business being in his field.

Fivefold ministers are invited into a ministry field

As a fivefold minister, the only way I can effectively minister in another sphere of responsibility is when I'm invited. When I'm invited into their field, I need to understand and acknowledge that someone else has final authority over this field. For a fivefold minister, probably 95 percent of his ministry is in someone else's field. A fivefold translocal minister's attitude must always be one of, "We're here to help others build what the Holy Spirit is building. It is not about building our own ministry, it is about serving the Lord and serving this particular church, co-laboring with them in their field. They have final authority in their field." Approaching ministry with that attitude and understanding, helps the fivefold ministry to be an asset rather than a threat to a local leadership team.

Safety within the ministry field

One day I received a phone call from one of our senior pastors in our worldwide network of churches. He mentioned that a fivefold translocal minister, who was not part of our family of churches, was speaking and ministering at some of the churches within our network, and he was in the midst of going through a second divorce. Since one of the capacities in which I serve our family of churches is that of an overseer, I knew it was my responsibility to inform the leaders of our churches of the situation. While my intent was not to bring embarrassment or harm to the fivefold translocal minister, I knew that I had a responsibility to the leaders for which I was responsible.

I received the name and contact information of this fivefold translocal minister and proceeded to give him a call because I wanted to be candid in all my communication, plus I wanted to make sure that the assessment of his marital status was true and accurate. He told me that he was indeed going through a difficult time in his marriage and contemplating divorce. I encouraged him to step back from ministry and focus on his relationship with his wife because that is the advice I would give to a fivefold minister under my oversight. I firmly believe that if a leader is at a desperate place in his marriage, he should pull back from ministry in order to take time to work at his relationship with his spouse. After the relationship is healed, and only then, do I advise that he return to ministry.

He told me that the leaders who give him oversight have been in communication with him, and while they acknowledge that his ministry schedule had been somewhat influential in the breakdown of his marriage, they encouraged him to continue to stay out there and minister.

Although I did not say it, I thought to myself, "In the meantime, your marriage is falling apart."

I ended our conversation by saying that I did not have the responsibility or authority in his life to tell him what to do, but I did have a responsibility for the churches that I give oversight to. I also told him that I could not tell our leaders that they could not invite him into their churches to minister—that would be controlling—but

I did need to be open and honest and inform them what I knew concerning his marital status. They could then be allowed to make their own decision.

My responsibility in my field of ministry is to look out for the safety of those in our network of churches. I would have defrauded them by not telling them the fivefold minister was going through a divorce. My field of ministry did not include his personal life, but it did include the lives of people that he was ministering to within our network of churches. He was stepping into my field of ministry, and I was responsible for it.

In summary, fields of ministry are not in place to hold a fivefold minister back. They are there for his protection because within his field he has an anointing from God. When he steps outside of his sphere of ministry, he begins to lose some of the anointing. When he honors those whom the Lord places in charge, he is honoring the Lord. When he honors the Lord, favor and anointing rest upon the fivefold minister.

CHAPTER 12

Qualifications of the Fivefold Minister

Those who have had longevity in the fivefold ministry have made character qualifications a priority. Like Stephen, they are full of faith;[1] they are those who "have been with Jesus"[2] and who have learned the secret of Matthew 20:25—whoever wants to be great must be the servant of all. Jesus is by nature a servant and He looks for those who have a servant's heart.

He is not looking for those who are out to make a name for themselves or build a ministry for themselves. He is looking for individuals who are sold out to Him and love Him with their whole heart and want to advance the kingdom of God regardless of the cost. Receiving accolades is not part of their thinking process— theirs is looking to see the kingdom move forward, so that people are blessed by God and walking in the same obedience that they have come to love. In other words, they are full of God's character. As any other leader in the body of Christ, their character plays a key role in releasing them into the fivefold ministry.

Character is not a qualification for discipleship but it is always a qualifier for those in leadership roles. Jesus took the twelve "rough and ready" disciples, discipled them for three years, filled them with His Holy Spirit on the day of Pentecost, and then released them to be world changers. They turned their world upside down and had the character to withstand the ridicule and abuse as well as the praise and adoration that came to them at various stages of their experience. They were able to go the distance and finish well. Finishing well should be the desire of everyone in leadership.

In today's culture we hear of leaders who had a tremendous anointing but did not have the character to handle that kind of anointing and fell by the wayside. I find it incredibly disheartening to hear about this person falling into immorality, that person getting caught in a compromising situation, and another individual no longer living the life that he taught so many others to live.

It is critical that leaders develop the character that the Lord lays out for them in His family. Otherwise the pressure, fame and demands of ministry cause them to stumble and fall and cause others to fall as well. As a leader, I want to be listed with those who ran well and who finished well. Godly character is the key to making that a reality.

Character comes first

Jesus placed a lot of emphasis on character. Putting a stronger emphasis on an individual's anointing and gift causes us to become enamored of the gift, and we forget to look at character. Sometimes because of the gift we overlook a character flaw, carelessly thinking that the gift and anointing make up for it. We think, "After all, if the Lord saw fit to give the individual the gift, who am I to question his character?"

However, the Bible says, "For the gifts and the calling of God are irrevocable…" (Romans 11:29). God decides whom to give gifts to, and it is up to us to submit ourselves to His discipline and accountability in order to grow in God's character so we can handle all that the gift brings us.

It is sad, but true, that some gifted and anointed fivefold leaders hide behind the "do not touch the Lord's anointed" verse (Psalm 105:15) which they use to silence people from questioning or criticizing them. Their character lacks substance, but they think that having a unique gift and calling entitles them to unconditional authority and special privileges.

Instead of drawing others closer to the Lord, building them up in the power of His might and grounding them in the Word of the Lord, they claim to be beyond criticism. This turns people off regarding the things of the Spirit, including the gift the Lord has given them. People will rightly say, "If that is the Lord, I don't want any part of that."

I was talking to a senior pastor one time who shared this story with me. He had contacted a minister to speak at his church. After the date was set and commitments were made, the minister began laying down requirements necessary for him to come. A certain kind of car was needed to pick him up at the airport, he needed to stay at a particular hotel with top-notch service, and on and on the list went.

After the individual ministered, the senior pastor received a love offering for him and presented him with a check as he was leaving. Since this was a sizable congregation, it was a very large check, more than "paying" him for services rendered.

Later on in the evening, the minister called the senior pastor and wanted to know where the rest of his payment was. He wasn't satisfied with the love offering. Now, if you were that senior pastor, would you want to have that individual back to minister again? I don't think so.

This minister was more concerned about building his own ministry than building the local church. A lack of character like this will eventually catch up with him. If we admit it, for the right price, we can get most any person who claims to have an anointing or gift mix to come to our church to minister. Their ministry, however, may be a flash in the pan and probably will not produce any measurable long term fruit.

I am not suggesting by this story that we should not pay fivefold ministers. On the contrary, the Bible says that a workman is worthy of his hire, whether it is my mechanic working on my car or a fivefold translocal minister imparting into my congregation. They should be paid and paid well. But payment is not the motivation of the fivefold minister. Building the kingdom is the motivation and drive behind his ministry.

Character defined

An honorable character is of utmost importance before being released into the fivefold ministry. Otherwise we will sabotage the very thing that the Lord wants us to do.

There is a short chapter in Psalms that deals entirely with character. These five powerful verses tell of the actions that come from having godly character.

> Lord, who may abide in Your tabernacle? Who may dwell in Your holy hill? He who walks uprightly, and works righteousness, and speaks the truth in his heart; He who does not backbite with his tongue, nor does evil to his neighbor, nor does he take up a reproach against his friend; In whose eyes a vile person is despised, but he honors those who fear the Lord; He who swears to his own hurt and does not change; He who does not put out his money at usury, nor does he take a bribe against the innocent. He who does these things shall never be moved. (Psalm 15:1-5 NKJV)

Please note that some of the following material in this chapter is taken from the book *The Biblical Role of Elders in Today's Church* by Larry Kreider, Ron Myer, Steve Prokopchak and Brian Sauder.

Character qualifications

In 1 Timothy 3:1-7, we find the specific character qualifications for "overseers." While fivefold ministers are not necessarily overseers, there is a similar test of character that has to be evident in their lives.

Here is a trustworthy saying: If anyone sets his heart on being an overseer, he desires a noble task. Now the overseer must be above reproach, the husband of but one wife, temperate, self-controlled, respectable, hospitable, able to teach, not given to drunkenness, not violent but gentle, not quarrelsome, not a lover of money. He must manage his own family well and see that his children obey him with proper respect. (If anyone does not know how to manage his own family, how can he take care of God's church?) He must not be a recent convert, or he may become conceited and fall under the same judgment as the devil. He must also have a good reputation with outsiders, so that he will not fall into disgrace and into the devil's trap.

To serve the church, a fivefold ministry leader
...is willing

An evidence of God's calling a person to serve is the presence of a desire or passion. This is not a human ambition; it is a calling from God—a deep desire and compulsion to lovingly serve the Lord's people. A fivefold minister's motivation is pure. It is not his ambition being worked out in a spiritual atmosphere where he can hide his true motivation. He is doing it because it is the Lord's call on his life. He loves the Lord and God's family. He desires to see the body of Christ strengthened. He would never knowingly do something that would bring disgrace or harm to the family or those in it.

...is above reproach

"Being above reproach" is not referring to perfection. Paul was calling attention to a person's reputation. A fivefold minister lives his life in such a way that no one can legitimately find fault with him. He is free from the taint of scandal and accusation[3] and has unquestionable integrity. If people look at his life and try to find something they can use against him, they will find it difficult, because he is blameless and above reproach. His character sets an example for all to follow. A man's reputation will go before him. A fivefold translocal minister must be above reproach because his is a traveling ministry; his reputation travels to the place before he does, and in many cases his reputation is part of the reason he is being invited.

...is the husband of one wife

The Greek translates this as a "one woman man." He maintains God's standard of morality. This passage in 1 Timothy 3:2 is sometimes used as proof text that a divorced person cannot serve as a fivefold minister in the church. However, if we look at the time it was written, we see that some of the converted Jews still had several wives as permitted under Semitic Law. It was this practice of having multiple wives that was being discouraged at the time of Christ, hence the reference to "being the husband of one wife." When he came to Christ, the new convert was faced with a new standard of morality—God's standard. The same standard applied for any Christian woman. She too was to be faithful to one husband.

The real question today is, "Can a previously divorced person serve in any capacity of leadership?" We believe they can. We have chosen to address each person who has divorced individually. There are far too many different circumstances and situations to make a sweeping rule. While every divorce is the result of sin, not every divorce is sinful. There are those who have been abandoned and had no choice to divorce or not to divorce. Their mates left them. We choose to consider each situation separately by praying, fasting and doing whatever it takes to hear from God about His desire to use a divorced potential leader. The key here is if the individual acknowledges that divorce is sin. I know some people who have gone through some very painful situations and they hate divorce because they have seen the destruction it can bring. Redemptively, they share their testimony with others to encourage them to continue to work through broken relationships with the goal of restoration. God is a

God of restoration. Along with that, I believe that for a Christian, initiating a divorce is not an option. God is a God of reconciliation and everything possible must be done to save that marriage relationship.

...is temperate; self-controlled

Self-control consists of the right use of one's will under the controlling power and performance of the Holy Spirit. It must be an outgrowth of the Spirit's working "both to will and to do of His good pleasure."[4]

Fivefold translocal ministers are disciplined people. They are able to control their desires and impulses. I try to not be brought under the control of anything. If I'm drinking too much coffee, I stop for days so that I am not being controlled by it. I figure that if I cannot go through a day without some specific thing, I am under its control. Of course I do not mean specific medications that are needed to stay healthy. I am talking about having controls on the appetites of my life.

All of us have appetites and ambitions that need to be under the Lord's control. Sampson lost his valid leadership anointing because he couldn't control his sexual appetite. Moses didn't fulfill his destiny to go into the Promised Land because he could not deal effectively with anger in his life. These examples are written for our benefit so that we can learn from them.

...is respectable

The Greek word translated "respectable" is *kosmios*. The English word "cosmetics" comes from the same root word. In Titus 2:10, the verb *kosmeo* is translated "to adorn."

In his book, *Leaders on Leadership*, Gene Getz tells a personal story of purchasing a house in a new neighborhood whose previous owner was a Christian minister. In this particular community, everyone kept their lawns well-manicured, except for the previous owner—the minister who allowed his expansive lawn to become a weedy hay field. After Getz, a minister himself, moved into the neighborhood, it took months for him and his family to build bridges with their neighbors because everyone was convinced all ministers were a bad lot—unconcerned and irresponsible. But they won their neighbors' respect by diligently and consistently keeping their property manicured and orderly. They could once again "adorn" the gospel of Christ by living a life-style that properly corresponded with the character of God.[5]

...is hospitable

Quite simply, "being hospitable" means "being fond of guests." The home of a church leader is an open home where people of all kinds feel welcome. A fivefold leader maintains a gracious and generous attitude toward others. Those in the fivefold ministry are willing to help, to come to others' aid; they enjoy associating with others.

When I was a senior elder I realized that hospitality was lacking in my church. How could I motivate people to be "fond of guests?" One Saturday at about four o'clock in the afternoon, I had a spontaneous idea, "Wouldn't it be really neat to have a bunch of people over for lunch tomorrow?" I asked my wife, Bonnie. "I am thinking that about forty people would be a good number," I continued.

Bonnie sort of gasped, and caught her breath. "That's a great idea, honey, and *you* can do it!" Bonnie's less than enthusiastic response did not deter my last-minute idea. I decided I was up for the challenge!

I rushed off to the soon-to-close grocery store and headed for the meat counter. I asked how much ham I needed for sandwiches to feed forty people. I then went to the "institution aisle" where they sold everything in larger quantities and bought several large cans of soup (I didn't know Campbells came in cans that large), two gallon cans of fruit salad, celery, several large bags of chips and a large amount of ice-cream. I ended up spending $1.65 per person.

On Sunday, after the service, I asked forty people to raise their hands if they wanted to come for lunch that day. I had no problem quickly recruiting people for a free lunch! Before they ate, I read Acts 2:46-47. "They ate their food with gladness and simplicity of heart." The point I was trying to make was that it doesn't take a fancy spread to be hospitable. It just takes time and a little bit of food. Several times over the next few months, I asked people from the congregation to come for lunch. One Sunday we had as many as sixty-three.

After a number of weeks of this, the cashier at the grocery store became curious. When I told her I was having forty people from my church over for lunch, she wanted to know where my church met! So you see, hospitality is not about putting out a four-course meal. Hospitality is simply inviting people into your life and home. Be warned, this can be habit-forming and highly contagious!

...has the ability to teach

This does not necessarily mean that all fivefold leaders have the gift of teaching or are great orators and speakers. Rather it implies they have the ability to communicate God's Word so that they can help others. Some fivefold ministry leaders are gifted to teach large groups, while others are gifted to teach one-on-one in a mentoring type relationship.

Fivefold ministers know the truth of God's Word well enough to be able to confront and admonish others when needed. They cannot teach what they do not know. "He must hold firmly to the trustworthy message as it has been taught, so that he can encourage others by sound doctrine and refute those who oppose it."[6] Remember part of their goal is to keep the body from being tossed to and fro by every wind of doctrine. They can only do that if they have a firm understanding of the word themselves.

Fivefold leaders are capable of teaching in a language people understand, reaching and connecting with their target audience.

They have a compulsion to pass on to others what they have learned. They have a genuine love for God's Word and a desire to impart it to others. When they know and can see that people are receiving the Word, it is like a refreshing wind to their spirit, and it energizes them.

...is not given to drunkenness

"Not given to drunkenness" literally means "not tarrying at wine." Fivefold leaders are not infatuated with alcoholic beverages and defiled by the life-style often associated with drinking. They have an exemplary life-style that is without the negative influence of alcohol or intemperance. "Do not get drunk on wine, which leads to debauchery. Instead, be filled with the Spirit."[7] It is always wrong to be addicted to anything. This includes wine, drugs, sex and even food.[8]

...is not overbearing, but humble

A fivefold leader must be selfless. He is not self-willed and arrogant.[9] His desire is for the people to be all they can be in God. He gives of himself for those in his care.

Fivefold leaders know that their dependence is totally on God. This keeps them walking in humility, rather than lording it over others.

Prestige and the desire to be admired and respected can overshadow a fivefold leader's ministry. Proverbs 8:13 tells us that God hates pride. Pride is at the center of "selfish ambition" according to James 3:16. Selfish ambition prompts us to promote our own interests, and we start to believe in our own merit, superiority and accomplishments. This verse goes on to say that selfish ambition leads to "every evil practice." Humility, as opposed to selfish ambition, causes us to consider others as better than ourselves.[10] A fivefold minister knows where his gift comes from and he is totally dependent on Jesus for that gift. He knows the gift originated from Jesus and is a gift to be used on others.

...is not quick tempered or quarrelsome

Fivefold leaders are not cranky or irritable and are not quick to get in verbal disputes. They do not lose their tempers and react when they are challenged or irritated. If they quickly become angry, they will make matters worse when dealing with conflicts. This makes reconciliation difficult. James gives this timely advice: "My dear brothers, take note of this: Everyone should be quick to listen, slow to speak and slow to become angry."[11] Those in the fivefold ministry are well-balanced in judgment, not impulsive or given to extremes.

They need to be persons of peace, not pushy or hard to get along with. They are ready to answer questions and quick to share what they understand, but they are not prone to get into long debates on frivolous issues.

...is gentle, not violent

A fivefold leader maintains relational integrity. He does not use force of character to get his way. He is not a bully in his relationships with others. Even under provocation, he does not strike out at people who try his patience. Fivefold leaders are courteous and considerate of others, in addition to being patient, kind, considerate, forbearing and not easily disturbed. They are individuals who are willing to yield or concede in a matter without compromising the truth.

Sheep must be led, not driven. I once led a meeting with a fivefold senior pastor and his team who were working through some difficult issues. At one point, the pastor responded to one disgruntled member of his team by saying, "I think you need to respond better to the prodding of your pastor. You really should learn to listen to my prodding."

I made a mental note of his statement and later confronted the pastor alone, "You know, brother, I think that it is 'goats' that need to be prodded," I reminded him. "As a shepherd, remember that sheep must be led." Being gentle means we are forbearing and patient. That's how Jesus deals with us. A fivefold leader's greatest weapon is love.

...is free from the love of money

A fivefold leader is free of greed. He is free of the love of money and the things that money can obtain. He believes money is a tool for God to use to bless others and is not to be hoarded. I like what a man of God said years ago and it always stuck with me, "If you teach your children one thing, teach them to be generous." When you have lost your ability to give, you have lost a major portion of the kingdom.

A fivefold leader is not out for personal gain or profit as a result of serving in the fivefold ministry. In the New Testament, it appears that certain leaders were financially supported in their work.[12] The churches were probably generous in their support which could lead one to be tempted to serve for the money.

Leaders are examples of how to honestly earn, spend and save money. They tithe to the local church that they are part of and give generously in a way that honors the kingdom of God and values the flock.

...is able to manage his own house well

A natural father has strong ties with his children and "manages" them so his children are not wild and unruly. He disciplines and trains them with dignity and respect. Children will want to do what is right because they respect and love their parents.

Fivefold leaders tenderly care for people so they are encouraged to move ahead with common purposes and goals. Parents make decisions that are best for the family. The same is true of fivefold leaders. They make decisions that are not always based on their own preferences but that are best for the church as a whole. When I minister at another leader's church, I say, "I want to accomplish what the Holy Spirit wants to accomplish today, and if He can accomplish it without me speaking, that's even better yet."

...has a good reputation with those outside the body

Leaders have good testimonies with the unsaved and stay away from compromising circumstances. "Live such good lives among the pagans that, though they accuse you of doing wrong, they may see your good deeds and glorify God on the day he visits us."[13]

One time I spoke quite directly to an unsaved individual who had taken advantage of me, lied to me, and furthermore would not acknowledge it. I was firm (perhaps "righteously indignant") and spoke my mind. However, when I walked away, I had to ask myself this question, "Could I have followed up that confrontation by witnessing to that individual, or was I too upset?" As a Christian and fivefold leader, I learned a hard lesson that day. I realized I would have to make some attitude adjustments.

Leaders have a "soundness of speech that cannot be condemned, so that those who oppose you may be ashamed because they have nothing bad to say about [you]."[14]

...loves what is good

God is good, therefore a fivefold minister's desires are focused on the good things of God. He is a godly person, hates sin and has a compassion for those whose lives are entangled by sin. With a no nonsense approach to sin, he takes a clear stand on sin issues because he loves that which is good and he hates that which is evil.

Fivefold ministers enjoy seeing the enemy defeated in others' lives. When someone else, individually or as a congregation, experiences victory, they experience victory. They see the good in others and in situations that are less than desirable. Since they see some of the negative things within the church, they also have the ability to see the good that can come out of these situations. They have a strong desire to see others succeed. They know that as others in the church succeed, they in turn succeed!

Because they frequently travel, they experience a wide range of situations, and not everything that they witness is good. They see some of the flaws in the body of Christ because they are "up close." But they never use this knowledge to shed a bad light on the body of Christ. They do not repeat things that should not be mentioned to others who are not part of the problem or solution. Philippians 4:8 is their guide: "Finally, brethren, whatever things are true, whatever things are noble, whatever things are just, whatever things are pure, whatever things are lovely, whatever things are of good report, if there is any virtue and if there is anything praiseworthy—meditate on these things" (NKJV).

...is upright; holy

Being upright and holy is doing what is right in God's sight regardless of the circumstances. It is doing right even when no one is looking or listening. It is having a heart that is pleasing to God. David said, "As the deer pants for streams of water, so my soul pants for you, O God."[15] That is holiness.

Fivefold leaders follow through on commitments, making good their word, even if it costs them financially. David said in Psalm 15, "He who swears to his own hurt...." In other words, I cannot violate an agreement simply because it will be a loss to me. Otherwise, the name of the Lord will be tainted.

If there are changes that need to be made, a fivefold leader appeals to the ones to whom they made the commitment, asking to be released or readjusted so as not to cause a problem, because they are there to serve.

Every year I travel both nationally and internationally. One year, I was stretched in my travel both physically and monetarily. It would have been easier emotionally, physically and financially to gracefully bow out of a trip or two at the end of the year. But I had given my word that I would come, and they were expecting me. I felt I needed to honor my commitment to be there.

Does that mean that I can never say "no" to a previously promised engagement? Not really. For example, last year I was asked to travel to Africa two different times by two different leaders. They wanted me to minister at two of their church anniversary celebrations in different locations on the continent. I knew that I would not be able to go both times, so we settled on the one anniversary celebration.

It wasn't long before I began to have second thoughts about going. I mentioned this to the leader in Africa and asked if it would be okay for me to take some more time to think and pray about it. He agreed. I presented my dilemma to my personal intercessors, asking them to pray about my trip to Africa. Before long my lead intercessor pulled me aside and said she heard a clear "no" concerning the trip to Africa. Shortly thereafter, two more intercessors contacted me and said that each time they had prayed they felt a caution in their spirits about my trip to Africa and that I should not go.

Finally, I talked to my overseer and explained the situation. We agreed that with three of my intercessors saying I should not go, it would be foolish for me to do so. I then contacted the leaders in Africa explaining what had transpired, and they agreed that it would be unwise for me to come. In this case, I made sure that I heard God and made good on my word.

...is not a new convert

Fivefold leaders should not be newly saved but have a history with God. When spiritual babies are given adult roles, they may become conceited. Spiritual growth should always precede responsibility.

Healthy leaders depend on God's grace and power to do the job assigned to them. Leading a small group can be a great training ground for a future fivefold ministry leader. If we are faithful in little, we will be faithful in much.[16]

There is no chronological age requirement for a fivefold leader, but maturity can be developed through life experiences. A. W. Tozer said; "It is not life's circumstances that make the man, it is man's response to life's circumstances that determine what kind of man he will become." A mature fivefold minister has learned how to respond properly to life's circumstances over the years.

...is willing to be tested

A leader realizes that there will be tests as the Bible says "...many are called, but few are chosen."[17] Many leaders who are rightly called by God fail the test of leadership and are no longer in leadership today. We learn from James 1:2-4 that the trials of life will either draw us closer to Jesus or drive us away from Jesus. God allows fivefold ministers to go through tests to see how they will respond under pressure. By their response, they either qualify or disqualify themselves.

I used to be in a farm partnership that did testing of new prototype farm equipment. The engineers who worked in the production room first put the equipment through their tests, and then they gave it to farmers like me who subjected it to a genuine field test. If the engineers said the machine would work in dry conditions, I also tested it in wet conditions. What good is a machine that only works in the best of conditions? I wanted to know what it would do in the worst conditions. Similarly, God allows us to be tested so that we have the opportunity to respond in a godly manner, passing the test.

In the church, leaders are sometimes harshly tested. When the pressure is on, what will they do? The true test of a leader is the way he responds and reacts to adverse situations.

When my youngest son was born, he remained in the neonatal intensive care unit in the hospital for a harrowing nine days. I had one thought in mind—to get my son out of there with a clean bill of health. On the fourth day, as I entered the unit, the Holy Spirit spoke to me and said, "You know you are missing it." I thought He was going to give me a new strategy to pray so that my son could be healed faster. What the spirit of the Lord spoke to my heart was this. "You are so concerned about your own needs that you are totally missing all of the hurting people around you." From that day on, I entered the hospital with a new focus—to notice and reach out to those around me who also had critical family health issues to face. I was not the only one with problems!

The truth is that there are a lot of things going on that are much bigger than we can see in any given situation. Wherever you are and whatever you are going through today is training for what the Lord has for you tomorrow!

...has the heart of a servant

Jesus by nature is a servant and He is looking for those who have a servant's heart.[18] A servant does not care about his own well being as much as he does about the one that he is serving. Jesus is our ultimate role model for leadership. He led by being a servant to all those around Him. He knew who He was because of His intimate relationship with His Father, and out of that relationship, He ministered to others' needs. From God's perspective, leaders and servants are synonymous in the body of Christ. In the world's system, leaders are expected to dominate those under them, but God has called leaders to follow the example of His Son, and be servants. My sense of value and worth cannot come from what I do or who I am serving, it comes from me knowing who I am and more importantly from the fact that when I am serving another individual I am really serving the Lord.

...is full of the Holy Spirit

The qualifications for a leader are challenging, and in fact, daunting. Without the Holy Spirit on whom to depend a leader cannot succeed! It is only by being full of the Holy Spirit's power that anyone, including fivefold ministers, can walk in victory and live the overcoming life. "So I say, live by the Spirit, and you will not gratify the desires of the sinful nature."[19] When we try to lead in our own strength, we can easily fall flat on our faces, but being full of the Holy Spirit will empower us to do what we can't muster up on our own!

...knows he is called by God

God sovereignly calls a fivefold minister into His service. If God calls, He equips the individual for the task because the Lord "...has saved us and called us to a holy life—not because of anything we have done but because of his own purpose and grace."[20]

A fivefold minister knows that God has called him, not man. If he is appointed without God's affirmation in his spirit, he will not have the grace from God to face the hard times, and the good times will be meaningless to him. Paul was clear about his calling to spiritual leadership—he knew that God had called him.[21] Because he knew it was the Lord that called him, it was up to the Lord to prepare the way for him.

Sometimes we can run ahead of the Lord and try to make a way for ourselves. Proverbs says a man's gift makes room for him. It doesn't say a man should make room for his gift. When you know you are called by the Lord, you do not have to strive to make something happen, you just relax in the Lord, allow Him to lead you, and it will happen. I like what William Carey said many years ago. "Expect great things from God; attempt great things for God." There is a role that He plays, but there is action that is required on our part to bring about greater honor, praise and glory to Him.

...is in love with Jesus

Fivefold ministers love Jesus and see others through the filter of His love. They know that Jesus loves them passionately and unconditionally and extends His lavish love to others.

People feel comfortable around godly leaders because they are able to relate to people from all walks of life. One time, a young man with a head of teased hair, dyed blue, came into a service I was leading. After the service, I talked to him at length showing genuine love and concern. I am always drawn to those who are different, who stand out. I like to say "hi" to them on the street, and I have found that almost without exception, people are all pretty much the same. They all have fears, hurts, needs, and are longing for someone to accept them. As I was talking to this young man, I couldn't help but wonder what he was trying to communicate through his dress. I was genuinely interested in him as an individual and took the time necessary to communicate that to him. Later, the young man told the friend who brought him how impressed he was that a church leader treated him as a normal human being. What surprised him the most was that I was able to look beyond his rather unusual hairstyle to see the person inside showing him value by looking him in the eyes the whole time we talked.

I'm convinced that many people with their outrageous dress are really just saying, "Please notice me." One of the worse things we can do is ignore them. Show them some attention, let them know that you care about them and Jesus does too!

...has endurance

A fivefold minister sees the big picture and does not give up easily when the going gets tough. "Therefore, since we are surrounded by such a great cloud of witnesses, let us throw off everything that hinders and the sin that so easily entangles, and let us run with perseverance the race marked out for us."[22]

The Christian life is to be run in such a way as to get the prize. "Do you not know that in a race all the runners run, but only one gets the prize? Run in such a way as to get the prize."[23] A fivefold minister stays in the race and does not get sidelined by problems life throws at him. One of the greatest acts of spiritual warfare is to not quit, to keep pressing on to the end.

Am I qualified?

After all of these qualifications, we may ask ourselves whether anyone is ever fully qualified. This is a pretty big bill to fill. I know for me personally, I haven't fully arrived at all of these areas, but I am headed in the right direction. The key is that the fivefold person is accountable in each of these areas. He is open to correction and adjustment and lives his life in such a way that he is approachable with those to whom he has submitted his life. I try to make it easy for those to whom I am submitted. Rather than wait for them to come to me, I ask them from time to time whether they have input for my life, especially concerning the areas that I may be weak in.

As we close this chapter, I would like to mention one more thing. One of the dangers for a fivefold minister, when the Lord starts to use him in greater ways, is for him to begin to think he is something special, above the rest of the crowd. The truth is we are all special in the eyes of the Lord. I like to tell people that when the Lord starts to use them, they are really "up there." In fact, they are right up there—with Balaam's donkey! The Lord used a lowly donkey to speak His word to Balaam. The Lord can use anyone and anything at anytime to accomplish His purposes, to speak His heart and to bring input and influence into a situation. I said it at the beginning of this chapter, and it bears repeating, "Character is a qualifier to be in a place of leadership."

CHAPTER 13

Ministry Motivation

Sometimes, as leaders, ministry can go to our heads. We become more excited about *ministry* than the One for whom we are ministering.

When the seventy disciples in Luke 10 returned to Jesus exuberant with joy because "even the demons were subject" to them, Jesus rejoiced with them by saying, "I saw Satan fall like lightning...." Nevertheless, He also wanted them to keep a clear perspective, so He continued, "Do not rejoice in this that the spirits are subject to you, but rather rejoice that your names are written in heaven."

Jesus emphasized that the greatest cause for rejoicing was not the momentary victory over the supernatural, but the eternal triumph they had as citizens of heaven.

While we should be excited about what we do for Jesus in His name, our real joy is found in the fact that we are children of the King. Whether He decides to use us or not has little bearing on the fact that we are important in the kingdom and to the King.

If we begin to draw value and self-worth from our ministry rather than from Jesus, we have missed a major key in understanding the proper motivation for ministry. After a while, ministry begins to fill a void in our lives, and our motivation becomes tainted. Before long, we approach ministry from the perspective of what it does for us rather than obedience to the King. When we use ministry this way, people will feel devalued. When people feel devalued we have misrepresented the One who sent us. When we misrepresent the One who sent us, we have failed.

This point was driven home to me one time as I ministered in one of the world's developing countries to a very poor, ordinary-looking individual. The Lord spoke to my heart that this person was just as important in His sight as any prestigious, well-to-do individual that I had ever ministered to in my own country. When we have the perspective that *everyone* is important, loved and valued by the Lord, and that Jesus wants to minister to each individual, whether rich and good-looking or poor and plain-looking, we begin to understand that Jesus loves every person the same and desires to bless them.

God is watching you! Do you have a desire to be used of the Lord in great capacities? I do. I want to be used by Him in any way that He would see fit to advance His kingdom. God sees how we respond to individuals, situations and opportunities. Do we pray as fervently for the ordinary person as we do for the distinguished and renowned individual? Do we show the same compassion for the hurting person in a western nation as in a developing one? Do we minister wholeheartedly whether there are twenty-five in attendance or two hundred fifty? We should.

Mother Teresa's response to ministry was simple. She said, "We are called upon not to be successful but to be faithful." When we are involved in ministry, especially the fivefold ministry, since it represents Christ himself, obedience and faithfulness are the guiding forces in our entire ministry.

Why should an individual want to be a fivefold minister? Why should he desire to be in ministry? Let's look at four keys that should motivate us in ministry.

1. Understand that it is the Holy Spirit doing the work

This aspect alone keeps us humble as the Lord uses us in ministry. In Mark 16, the Great Commission commands believers to go into the entire world. As we go, the Lord promises great signs will follow us. When God begins to use us and pours out His Spirit, we cannot make the mistake of thinking we are overly important. Merely because we pray for someone and God answers by a display of His supernatural power does not mean we should begin to "think more highly of ourselves than we ought."[1] We are vessels of clay, and without the power of the Holy Spirit at work in our lives our efforts are ineffective. We need a clear understanding of grace. In his book *Living in the Grace of God*, Larry Kreider explains grace this way,

> Remember the grape-picking laborers in Matthew 20? They complained and wondered why everyone got paid the same for varying hours of labor because they didn't understand the grace of God. If we question why God gives some people greater talents and abilities than others, we have not understood the grace of God. If we think we are a better worship leader than Jim or a better teacher than Sally, we are falling short of God's grace.

> It is so important to refrain from comparing ourselves with others. We should only compare ourselves with the Word of God and allow the Word to dwell in us so we can live out the principles of grace in our lives. If we feel like we are doing better than others, we fall into pride. If we feel like we are doing worse than those around us, we can suffer from feelings of inferiority. When we compare ourselves to others, we are not wise, according to 2 Corinthians 10:12. Neither pride or inferiority are grace-filled responses.

> When God uses someone else for a certain ministry or responsibility and we are not called into action, how do we respond? When we begin to compare ourselves to other people, we are falling short of the grace of God. God is God. He knows best what we need. He may give somebody

one gift and another a different type of gift. Understanding and walking in the grace of God will permeate our total being and way of thinking. It changes our attitudes, causing us to want to grow up spiritually so that we can help and serve those around us.[2]

Jesus clearly told the disciples in John 14:10 that it is "...the Father, living in me, who is doing his work." When great things happen, it is the power of God working through us!

Jesus also said in Mark 16:17, that the miraculous will follow those who believe. I used to think that He was speaking of those who believed in the miraculous, and that is partially true.

However, I also believe that what Jesus was implying here is referenced back to John 14:10. When great things happen in ministry, it is because the Father is doing the work through us. We can never take credit for what God does. We are totally dependent on the Lord living in us to do anything.

There is safety and freedom in realizing that it is God doing the work and not ourselves. Think of it—if we do not take the credit when Jesus moves powerfully and changes a person's life, then we do not have to take the blame when nothing happens! That relieves all the pressure of ministry. I don't have to try and make something happen. If the Father isn't doing anything, I don't need to do anything. Sometimes we put so much pressure on ourselves. Christians are to enjoy life, to live it "abundantly" as Jesus said. If I am under pressure to perform in ministry, most of the fun of ministry is removed. After awhile, I will become a slave to the ministry by always trying to make something happen. True ministry is allowing the Holy Spirit to move through us.

As fivefold ministers, part of our ministry description is to create an atmosphere where the Holy Spirit can work or prepare people's hearts so that He can move freely in their lives, raising their expectations, desires and level of faith to the place where they are open and expecting to see God move. Only an insecure individual will try to draw people and ministry to themselves. Our goal as fivefold ministers should be to point people to Jesus, assisting Him in ministering to them. If the Lord can minister what He needs to minister to the individual without me, so much the better. People may forget what I tell them, but they are prone to remember what the Lord speaks to their hearts.

The number one motivation in ministry is to point people to Jesus so that He gets the credit for all the good that happens. Obviously, God uses people, and as a fivefold minister, it is truly a privilege and blessing to be used by the Lord in people's lives. All in all, my excitement comes not from the fact that I am the one ministering, but that the *Lord* is ministering to them.

2. Understand that our sole purpose is to please God

In addition to understanding that the Holy Spirit is doing the work and not us, we must be motivated in ministry to please God. Like Jesus, we can be at a place of security in our lives where praise and criticism have the same effect on us—nothing! I strive for that place of ministry! I am not there yet, but I want to be there. Jesus' sole purpose was to please God. "For I have come down from heaven not to do my will but to do the will of him who sent me."[3]

We see some of the most distressing verses in the Bible in John 12:42-43 where leaders were more concerned with what people thought than with pleasing God.

> Yet at the same time many even among the leaders believed in him. But because of the Pharisees they would not confess their faith for fear they would be put out of the synagogue; *for they loved praise from men more than praise from God.*

These individuals missed everything the Lord had for them because they were more concerned about what man thought than about what God thought.

In stark contrast, Paul and Barnabas are examples of those who were not concerned with what the people thought of them. They refused to receive the "praises of men" in Acts 14 when the miraculous happened and people were healed.

> When the crowd saw what Paul had done, they shouted in the Lycaonian language, "The gods have come down to us in human form!"...But when the apostles Barnabas and Paul heard of this, they tore their clothes and rushed out into the crowd, shouting: "Men, why are you doing this? We too are only men, human like you. We are bringing you good news, telling you to turn from these worthless things to the living God, who made heaven and earth and sea and everything in them."...Even with these words, they had difficulty keeping the crowd from sacrificing to them.

However, it is rather interesting to see what transpires just after the crowd wanted to worship them as gods. Verse 19 says:

> Then some Jews came from Antioch and Iconium and won the crowd over. They stoned Paul and dragged him outside the city, thinking he was dead.

One moment Paul and Barnabas were treated like gods, and the next Paul was stoned as a heretic. People are finicky. People left Jesus' ministry, and probably they will leave ours. That's why we cannot seek people's praises, but rather the Lord's. Whether they were admiring him or trying to kill him, Paul had the same abiding assurance. He was confident and secure in the fact that he was speaking the word of the Lord.

3. Understand that we must have the heart of a servant

Jesus condemned the self-seeking ambition of the Pharisees who brought attention to their position as leaders. He advocated a different way of thinking entirely by saying, "The greatest among you will be your servant."[4]

Ministry is not for "getting." Ministry is for "giving." If a leader is in the ministry for what it does for him, he is using ministry. If he is using ministry to fulfill his own needs, it will only be a matter of time until he begins to use the people he is ministering to. And when a leader begins using authority for his own benefit, it becomes abusive authority.

Serving is giving out of a posture of strength. Jesus served out of an inner strength. He knew who He was, where He was coming from and where He was going. He was totally confident and secure in who He was. A secure minister will serve in any way that is needed because he is secure. Servanthood is not a position, it is a condition and posture of the heart. I like what my friend Steve says about leadership, "Leadership is not the brass ring to be grasped, and once you have it you don't need to serve anymore. Serving is the very thing that gives you authority to be a leader. Once you lose your heart to serve, you have given up your right to be in authority."

Our need for security, fulfillment, a sense of accomplishment, success, appreciation, self-value and worth must come from God and our relationship with Him. It cannot come from titles, who we work for or what we do.

When Jesus washed His disciples' feet in John 13, He was really saying, "Do you know what I am doing? I am greater than you, but I am willing to serve you." Jesus wants us to follow His example.

The people God calls and places in leadership do not strive for a leadership position or title. However, once they have that role of authority, they do not back down, but assume the responsibility the Lord placed upon them and fulfill that call on their lives. Floyd McClung said one time, "If a person wants authority, don't give it to him. If he wants responsibility, give it to him with authority."

God is not looking for people who need authority to feel good about themselves, rather He is looking for people who feel good about themselves and want to help others in the name of Jesus.

Godly leadership is not something to be grasped, but once it is given, it is not to be taken lightly. Moses did not strive to lead the children of Israel. In fact he tried a number of times to get out of it citing numerous excuses to the point where God was upset with him. Have you ever done that? Have you ever tried to convince Jesus that He was asking the wrong thing of the wrong person? I have. Eventually, I learn to accept the things that the Lord is asking me to do, even though they may be stretching for me. I have found that pressure drives me to the Lord. When I am asked to do something that is beyond my natural capabilities or level of expertise, it causes me to pray more, spending more time at the feet of Jesus listening to His instructions. Ministry draws me to the Lord because I realize that without Him, I have no ministry.

While Moses did not seek out leadership, when it was given to him, he accepted it from the Lord as God's call on his life. Later, when Miriam and some others came to Moses and questioned his leadership, he did not relinquish his authority. He knew he had to fulfill God's call and stand his ground, even interceding for them and telling them not to rebel against the Lord.

Twice while I was preparing to minister, God spoke these words to my heart, "Get off the stage!" Both times, I knew the Lord was revealing to me that public ministry cannot be seen as something to strive for. People often idolize the on-stage ministry and think, "If only I can make it to that level, I will be of value." Certainly, powerful ministry often happens up front, but I have seen God move just as powerfully in a group of less than twenty-five people in a small room or during one-on-one ministry. It is not the size of the group or the place in the room that limits God. It is our understanding and expectation that God is drawn to the fanfare of public ministry.

Obviously there are different dynamics at work when there is a larger group meeting, but if we place our emphasis on the larger crowds, we are training people that the larger the crowd, the bigger and better the anointing. And that is not always the case.

God does not want to share His stage with anyone. I often tell our fivefold ministers that their private anointing is just as important as their ministry in public. They need to sense the Lord's presence when it is just them and the Lord without the crowd.

If fivefold ministers think that the best ministry happens on stage, it becomes a platform or a place of performance where people will notice them. With a place of performance comes an evaluation or rating. We begin to ask questions such as, "Was it good?" "Did you like it?" We become more concerned with what we look like, how the people will receive us, and what the people are thinking. This is a trap.

Instead, our primary questions should be, "Was it God?" "Did it minister God's heart to you?" "Was the message shared really what God wanted to communicate?"

Having the heart of a servant is willing to serve without recognition. Jesus said that even after we have done everything He has asked us to do, we have done nothing, really. Why? Because it is only what is our duty to do!

> Suppose one of you had a servant plowing or looking after the sheep. Would he say to the servant when he comes in from the field, "Come along now and sit down to eat"? Would he not rather say, "Prepare my supper, get yourself ready and wait on me while I eat and drink; after that you may eat and drink"? Would he thank the servant because he did what he was told to do? So you also, when you have done everything you were told to do, should say, "We are unworthy servants; we have only done our duty."[5]

Ministry is not a position to bring self-affirmation; it is a place of servanthood.

4. Understand that we must get the job done

If our ultimate motivation is to complete the job, then we will look for the best way for it to happen. I call this being "vision-driven." This is different from being "driven by the vision."

Being vision-driven is looking for the most effective way to get the job done using the most effective people to do it. The example that I often use is American football. Each team has one goal in mind—to get the pigskin to the other team's end zone. All the coaches, staff and players use the most effective way to see that vision accomplished. They are vision-driven. The field goal kicker does not approach the coach when the ball is on their own twenty-yard line and say, "Let me try a field goal. I hardly ever get a chance to kick a field goal. Let me in right now." That would be ludicrous. On the contrary, he might say to the coach, "Get it to the thirty-five-yard line, and I think I can get it in; get me to the twenty-yard line and I guarantee I will get points on the board."

Being driven by the vision is when the vision drives us to sacrifice things that the Lord is not asking us to sacrifice in order to fulfill that vision. Too often, things like health, family and relationships take a back seat to those who are driven by the ministry. Not that sacrifices do not need to be made, but we should not make sacrifices that the Lord isn't asking us to make.

We must listen closely to the Holy Spirit: He is vision-driven. He has a vision that will be fulfilled. One time I was ministering after a church service as people came forward for prayer. I started to pray for the next woman in line and heard the Holy Spirit say I should ask the pastor's wife of the church to come up and pray for this woman. I looked up to find that the pastor's wife was leaving the room, but I sent someone after her and asked her to come up front.

I really did not know why the Holy Spirit wanted to use her. Did she have a greater anointing to minister to this individual? Did God want to use her because she was feeling like she was a "nobody"? God did not reveal the "why" to me, but I knew this pastor's wife was the one who could "get the job done." I briefly prayed for her that a greater anointing would arise in her. It happened! There was a powerful manifestation as she prayed. The pastor's wife continued to pray for people needing prayer and God used her to complete what He wanted to do that morning. I did not need to be the one ministering; God can use others to get the job done!

Self-preservation causes a fivefold minister to say and do that which promotes himself and his ministry. If he feels threatened by those who seem more gifted or qualified, he may not ask them to minister. Self-preservation may hold him in a limbo state and hinder him from growing.

God wants us to be fruitful and continue to grow. It was self-preservation that caused the Pharisees to hate Jesus so much. They realized His teaching would take away their authority and control over the people, so they rose up against Him.

A friend of mine, Phil, often said, "Worth and value are not the same as level and function." Success is being what God created you to be. If God has called you to usher people to their seats every Sunday morning, your reward will be the same as the apostle who is sent to plant churches. It comes down to faithfulness and obedience. God rewards faithfulness. He sees our heart motivation and knows why we are doing what we are doing.

The Lord is glorified when we bear fruit—when we are doing what we were created to do. Whatever aspect of ministry, God is glorified when you fulfill that ministry. "This is to my Father's glory, that you bear much fruit, showing yourselves to be my disciples."[6]

We can be excited about ministry!

It is not wrong to feel good and be excited about ministry. We can be joyful about ministry because *people are pointed to Jesus.* We are not on stage, but instead Jesus is being lifted up and people are drawn to Him.

When ministry takes place, we can be excited because *people are ministered to by the Holy Spirit.* We begin to see the Holy Spirit working in their lives. The Holy Spirit can do it better than anyone.

Another thing that happens during ministry is that *the enemy is crushed.* When God invades someone's life, it brings tremendous joy because the kingdom of darkness receives a blow. That in itself should bring a resounding "yes!" in our spirits no matter who is getting credit for the ministry. When someone scores a touchdown, the whole team rejoices because they know that they win or lose as a team. As a team, they are vision-driven. If only we could grasp the same concept in the church!

CHAPTER 14

Financing the Fivefold

We have the vision, the qualifications, the affirmation of those who give oversight to our lives and the right motivation to do this thing called *fivefold ministry*. Now the big question is, how do we finance it?

It is easy if you are a pastor and lead a church; you have a constant flow of finances called *tithes* from which to draw and build. But what if you do not have a church?

I have just hit on the reason why there are many leaders with one of the fivefold gifts leading churches when they really aren't called to do it. They lead churches because it is the easiest way to finance their ministries of apostles, prophets, evangelists, pastors or teachers. They are not fulfilled at it, and may not have the governmental calling to lead, but it is one of the only mechanisms in place that works.

They know that if they were to step down from leading the church, their finances would dry up. Sometimes this even leads to fivefold ministers laying down their call. They still have the call and the anointing for that call; they just haven't a clue on how to make a living while doing it.

This is not an easy question to answer nor is it one to take lightly. If we truly want to see the fivefold ministry released in today's church, we must figure out how to finance these individuals. Obviously when someone is leading a church, the pressures of ministry can be greater and more demanding than someone who is a fivefold minister in the local congregation, but fivefold ministers still have bills to pay just like everyone else. They need gas for their car, food for their children and vacations just like the rest of us.

While I do not have all the answers, I believe I can at least give some insights that can help you get started. We are still trying to walk through this ourselves. In our movement of churches we have a number of fivefold ministers who are released throughout our network, but all of them are bi-vocational. We just do not have the finances to support them full time.

There is also a certain amount of what I would call "critical mass" that is necessary for someone to be supported full time for fivefold ministry. In other words, for a single church to support a fivefold minister, they would most likely need to be in the mega church size (over a thousand members) to be able to raise the finances because there are both more funds and a larger workload available. To be fully supported in a network of churches, there would need to be a large enough network to provide the finances.

What if you are not a part of a mega church or a large network of churches that can support you? There are other ways. In this chapter, we will soon explore several different options.

Our financial cups

For years Larry Kreider, who leads our family of churches, talked about what he calls our *financial cup*. This *cup* constitutes our financial needs for existence as an individual or as a family. Bonnie and I have a very real financial cup that needs to be filled every month so we can fulfill our commitments and covenants that we have made with our electric company, credit card company, insurance company, food store, garage and so on. We are in covenant with each of these businesses, promising that we will pay for the services that we use. I need my financial cup filled every month to see that happen.

A friend of mine, Gene, who has been used in a wonderful way in the business field and the church, said something to me some time ago that has really impacted my thinking. He said, "There are opportunities all around us. Opportunities to make money, opportunities to minister to people, opportunities to do all kinds of things, but we have to be willing to do it."

As Christians, we are all in full time ministry whether it is through our business, at our job, in our school, at our home in the neighborhood or leading a church. Our goal is to share the light of the gospel as we go about our daily lives. What is different for each of us is how our financial cup will be filled. When an individual is involved in ministry, like the fivefold minister, it is wise to think about having two cups filled: your family financial cup (the finances needed to live as a family), and your ministry expense cup (the finances needed to accomplish the ministry to which the Lord has called you).

Biblical precedent: Laborers should be supported

In Bible times, when oxen were driven back and forth over the threshing floor so they could stamp out the grain from the chaff, they were allowed to eat of the fruits of their labors. In some kinds of labor the oxen were muzzled, but Old Testament law required that on the threshing floor, which required repetitious and continuous labor, the oxen should be rewarded. "Do not muzzle an ox while it is treading out the grain."[1]

Paul quotes this law both in 1 Corinthians 9:9 and 1 Timothy 5:18, showing that God did not appoint it for the sake of oxen alone, but that every laborer is worthy of his hire. We willingly pay the car mechanic and the doctor for their services, so we should gladly reward those who labor for the good of our souls.

For it is written in the Law of Moses: "Do not muzzle an ox while it is treading out the grain." Is it about oxen that

God is concerned? Surely he says this for us, doesn't he? Yes, this was written for us, because when the plowman plows and the thresher threshes, they ought to do so in the hope of sharing in the harvest. If we have sown spiritual seed among you, is it too much if we reap a material harvest from you? If others have this right of support from you, shouldn't we have it all the more?

But we did not use this right. On the contrary, we put up with anything rather than hinder the gospel of Christ. Don't you know that those who work in the temple get their food from the temple and those who serve at the altar share in what is offered on the altar? In the same way, the Lord has commanded that those who preach the gospel should receive their living from the gospel.[2]

It is clear from this passage that Paul believed that those who labored in the service of God should have competent support. In 1 Timothy 5:18, Paul again mentions the analogy between the oxen and the one who labors for the welfare of the church. Again, he says they should be given sufficient or appropriate recompense.

Potential sources of provision

Fivefold ministers are those who labor for the welfare of the church. They need to have a means of support to fill their cups. I believe their cups may be filled by a combination of sources. Here are some of the ways the Lord may choose to provide for them.

Tent-making

This type of provision is entirely funded by a person's own secular work. In Acts 18:1-3, we see that there was no church money supporting Paul at this time. He earned his income by his own labors: "...because he was a tentmaker as they were, he stayed and worked with them..." Tent-making is working at a job or business to earn income to finance a fivefold minister's family and the new church plant if he is planting a church.

I am currently writing this chapter while sitting in a flat in Sliven, Bulgaria. I have traveled here with a friend, Steve, and we have come to encourage the churches here to fulfill their God-given destiny. Steve leads a church in Ohio. But Steve doesn't take any finances from the budget of the church. His financial cup is filled by the business that he owns in part, a feed mill and grain storage facility. He leads the church, and the Lord provides financially for him through a tent-making job.

Bulgaria is a growing nation that is on the upsurge financially. Last night we were sitting with the leaders of the church here and Steve was talking with a young man about his financial needs. He naturally got around to asking him about the possibility of starting a business. The young man shared that this was something the Lord had been placing on his heart, but he wasn't sure how to go about it. Steve was able to give some insights, encouraging him that now is the time to start a business venture while the nation's economy is beginning to grow. He even sowed a small amount of money toward starting this young man's new business. It is a wide open opportunity before him. We are hearing more and more about how the Lord is beginning to supply the needs of those in ministry by new business ventures. It is something that the Holy Spirit is doing.

Support team of family and friends

With the extra manpower of Silas and Timothy arriving to help Paul in his work, in Acts 18, we notice that Paul shifts from full-time secular work to having his finances provided for him so that he could devote all his time to others. "When Silas and Timothy came from Macedonia, Paul devoted himself exclusively to preaching..." He could do this because additional breadwinners arrived, and they could pool their paychecks, so Paul would not have to work at a tent-making job. Paul now had a team supporting him financially while he ministered full-time.

In Luke 8:1-3, we read that Jesus had a team who supported Him from their substance. Many para-church ministries encourage missionaries and church planters to build a support team of family, friends and churches who give financially on a regular basis to support them in their calling and ministry. This is a scriptural way for the Lord to provide for the fivefold ministry.

Youth With A Mission has made this a very practical and effectual type of support. They call it "friend raising." The phrase is taken from a book by Betty Barnett on personal support raising entitled *Friend Raising*. The idea is to find others who believe in your calling and ministry, and give them an opportunity to sow into your life financially as you accomplish that ministry.

We must be careful here that we place our dependency entirely on the Lord and do not become dependent on others to supply our needs. We should not become Christian beggars, constantly asking people for finances. If the Lord is calling you to fivefold ministry, then He has a financial plan to see it happen without putting undue pressure or guilt on people to support you financially. I believe that you as an individual should be supplying at least some of your own finances, whether it is through a job or ministry work that you are paid for in order to generate some of your own support.

In this type of "friend support," some principles should be followed. There needs to be a communication link with those who are supporting you and the ministry that you are doing. We are all stewards of what the Lord has given us, and we are responsible to put our money into fruitful areas of ministry. Regular communication with updates and reporting ongoing vision are necessary to keep those supporting you aware of all that the Lord is doing in your life and the lives of those whom you are touching.

Supernatural provision

In Matthew 17:27, Peter found a coin in the mouth of a fish to pay his taxes and Jesus' taxes. This was not normal for Jesus' provision; however, the Lord did feed the 5,000 supernaturally. I have heard stories, although I have never experienced it personally, where the Lord has provided money spontaneously and supernaturally. We are not talking about an extra check in the mail, or someone coming up to you and handing you an envelope with money in it that you weren't expecting. While each of those is definitely provision from the Lord, we are talking about pure supernatural provision here. It is the kind of provision where the Lord provides money where there is no natural explanation for it, only God's supernatural provision. Fivefold ministers can expect that the Lord will provide finances supernaturally at times. Usually, it is for a specific need when there is nowhere else to turn for relief, and the Lord brings relief. While these times are amazing, it is very rare to live like this all of the time.

Local church support

In 2 Corinthians 8:3-4, a gift was given to Paul from the local church. Some fivefold ministers are blessed by the support of their local church as God's way of providing for them. We believe that everyone in the body of Christ needs to be committed to a local body of believers. It doesn't matter if it is a mico community (house church)[3] or a mega church—fivefold ministers should be a part of a local expression. If they are not connected to a local church, they can forget what body life is like with all of the challenges of ministry and life. They will feel and be detached, and their ministry will not be as relevant as it would be if they were part of a local expression.

A developing fivefold gift will first be acknowledged in the local church. It is in the environment of local church accountability that it is allowed to be tested, developed, mentored and matured. You wouldn't allow a surgeon to operate on you if he didn't have the proper training, mentoring and accountability of the medical board that brings correction to him if he makes mistakes.

Why would you allow a prophet to speak things into your life if he has not had the proper training, mentoring and accountability of a local church to bring correction and adjustment into his life?

It would be pure foolishness. I run into fivefold ministers like this from time to time as I travel to various parts of the world. They have a true gift but are not accountable anywhere, and they want to prophesy over me. I am guarded with those who cannot submit to a local church.

Conversely, if a fivefold minister *is* committed and loyal to a local congregation and has a valid developing ministry, I encourage the leadership of that local church to try to carve out some of their yearly budget for that individual. The fivefold minister, in turn, should make himself available to serve that leadership team in any way he can to enhance the ministry of the local church.

If you are reading this book and you are part of a church leadership team, I highly encourage you to pour some finances into the developing fivefold ministry. It does not always have to be in the form of a paycheck. There are many other ways that you can pour finances into the developing fivefold. Here are a few ideas:

Keep finances available in your church to bring in other fivefold ministers to train (invest in) your own developing fivefold ministers. Pay for a luncheon meeting, allowing plenty of time for questions and answers and impartation.

Have finances available to send the developing fivefold minister away to a seminar or conference pertaining to his specific gift.

Cover some travel expenses as he ministers in your small groups.

Pay for the fivefold minister to go on a two-night get-away to a hotel or retreat center to spend time alone with the Father. You are showing him that he is valuable and worth investing in.

Buy some teaching videos or audio tapes pertaining to their gifts and make them available. You are investing in the future.

All of these ways will show developing fivefold ministers that they are of value to you, you believe in developing the fivefold ministry, and that they are worth investing into.

Living from the gospel

Those who preach the gospel should live from the gospel, according to 1 Corinthians 9:7-14. Galatians 6:6 says, "Let him who is taught the word share in all good things with him who teaches."

There are some fivefold ministers who have taken the step of faith and gone on the road, so to speak. This concept may conjure up ideas of an evangelist in a white suit with a mailing list. He blows into town, teaches a powerful message, has people sign up for his newsletter and then they are on his mailing list for years as he continues to send them material asking for finances to support what he is doing in other parts of the world. While this is not inherently bad, the problem comes when people begin sending him their tithe money that should be going to the local church.

Although the fivefold minister will pray for us when we send him a contribution with a prayer request on it, he is not going to take our spiritual growth personally. If one of our children gets sick, we are not going to call him to meet us at the hospital.

We must be practical—a traveling fivefold minister cannot be our pastor, and we should be tithing to the storehouse, our local church, where we are receiving personal care and concern for our lives.

Certainly, the traveling fivefold minister who has lived from the gospel is worth investing in. A personal friend of mine, Dennis, is an example of a fivefold minister who lives exclusively from the gospel as a traveling prophetic minister for quite a number of years. He formerly pastored a church where the Lord began developing a prophetic gift in his life. As it continued to develop, he became more and more effective in ministry. It was clear that the Lord was doing something. He felt the Lord saying that it was time to turn the leadership of the church over to another individual and give all of his time to the prophetic ministry.

This is not an easy thing to do, especially if the fivefold minister will need to derive all of his support from his traveling ministry. It can be quite difficult to live on love offerings, unless you are drawing large crowds or ministering in mega churches that give sizable offerings and honorariums. What's more, a fivefold minister often ministers on one or two occasions on the weekend but his bills come in all week long.

In our network of churches, we believe that those who teach and preach should receive some sort of remuneration. While we do not pay a regular paycheck to a fivefold minister who is training us, we encourage churches to give either an honorarium or love offering to the individual. Whether the fivefold minister is ministering in a small group or a large congregation, an opportunity for people to sow into the individual should always be given. We need to be generous in blessing those who minister. In doing so, as leaders, we are teaching our people, by example, to give.

"Honor" given to a minister who is sent out

1 Timothy 5:17-18 tells us the laborer is worthy of his wages. Sometimes a local church leader will be supported as he ministers for a season in another part of the world. This, more or less, puts him in a *missionary* category. Because of their relationship with him and an affirmation of the gift, the church leadership team feels led of the Holy Spirit to continue to support the outgoing minister for a season of time. It is almost as if he is on staff with the local church. This can be for a short season or a longer period. Communication and relationship must be continued, and leadership teams should evaluate yearly those whom they are supporting and how much they give toward support. The minister is counting on that support, so if there is going to be a change, church leadership should make sure that they let the individual know in advance. Give them at least three months notice so they can make preparations for the change.

Inheritance

Proverbs 13:22 says a good man leaves an inheritance to his children's children. Some families have used inheritance money as God's provision to support them as short-term missionaries and church planters. I have a friend whose grandfather started a business years ago. It was very successful and my friend began to work for the company. A number of years ago, the company was sold. He received just a small percentage of the sale, but because the volume was so large he no longer needs to work a regular job. He still must mind his investments and make wise decisions on spending and investing, but he is free from punching a time-clock. He is using his time and energies in church planting and ministry.

Investments and business

In the Parable of the Talents in Matthew 25:14-18, Jesus brings home the point that we should be faithful and multiply the talents He has given us. Some successful business persons who have been blessed to use their talents wisely give a season of their lives to missions and church planting. I have worked with a number of pastors who have secular jobs and take little or no money from the budget of the church. The Lord just provides for them. Retired military personnel, teachers, government workers and others who have an opportunity to retire early, have at times used their pension to support themselves financially in church planting, fivefold ministry and missions. Because they are business owners, sometimes they have the flexibility that others who work for an hourly wage do not have. That is one of the blessings of owning a successful business. You can still be making money without being there around the clock. When I first planted a church, I did not take any finances. I was supported by the farm I owned. It was after I sold the farm that I began to receive finances from the church.

The ant method (work and save)

Proverbs 6:6-8 tells us that ants "labor hard in the summer, gathering food for the winter" (LB). Some individuals work hard and save for a season and then use the money that is saved to support themselves. I know of some fivefold ministers who work many years and get to a level financially that they now have financial freedom to go into full-time ministry. A case in point could be an owner of a company, who delegates others to run the business, leaving him with the flexibility to go into full- or part-time ministry. Or, someone who has a seasonal job can make a year's living in six months of the year and then can travel freely the remaining six months.

Count the cost

Common sense tells us that we must count the cost before starting a project.[4] Unmet expectations bring a death blow to many church planters, spiritual leaders, translocal fivefold ministries and missionaries. In light of this, the following questions may be of help to you as a fivefold minister to count the cost regarding how the Lord will fill your financial cup.

Lord, have you called me to be a translocal minister?

Lord, how do you desire to fill my cup?

Lord, what can I do now to start?

Am I willing to count the cost and "bear the cross"? (If God's choice of provision is not the same as yours, this may be your cross to bear.)

When one door of provision closes, am I willing to allow God to open another?

Some danger signs to avoid

Talking about finances is always an issue that is close to the heart of every individual because finances are such a vital part of our lives. When we discuss finances there are always some things that we need to be aware of because if they are not dealt with, they can cause us to stumble. Here are some danger signs to avoid:

Dictating to God how to fill your cup. If He is calling you to be a fivefold minister, then allow Him to tell you how He is planning on supporting you and your family while you do it. You will become frustrated and sometimes angry if the Lord doesn't come through in the way and method that you thought He should.

Comparing how God is filling your cup with how He fills others' cups. He is the supplier of our needs. Allow Him to do it in His fashion, according to His plan. Of course, you can observe how the Lord fills another person's cup to spark some creativity in your own life as to how the Lord wants to supply your needs.

Seeing one area of provision as more spiritual than another, and it becomes an idol in your heart. God can use any number of ways to fill your financial cup. One way is not more spiritual than another. You must weed out those sentiments before you are placed into fivefold ministry. If you trust any one area as being more spiritual, you get your eyes off of the Lord.

Not being willing to pay the "timing price." Often finances are used to tell *when* a ministry is to be launched. It is all part of the training as well. The Lord uses the process of filling our cup to prepare us spiritually for service. Our value system of finances may need to be overhauled, and it may take time to do that. Developing a financial track to fill our financial cups is always met with attack from the enemy. We need to know when we must stand against his devices and when it is purely the Lord saying, "It is not time yet, son."

Expecting another person, mission agency or church to provide the funds to fill your cup. Let's get it straight right now. Your trust and focus cannot be on other individuals. Sometimes we can look at successful businesspersons and think that they should be giving some of their money to us. When we begin to see others as our source, we take our eyes off of the Lord as our provider.

Jesus told His disciples not to be ashamed to earn their living from the gospel, "for the worker deserves his wages." I believe the Lord is giving fresh wisdom for many unique ways fivefold translocal ministers can be supported financially.

CHAPTER 15

Church Planting and the Fivefold

The model developed in the early church, according to the book of Acts, has the fivefold ministry intimately involved in church planting.[1] Where no church existed, the apostles preached the gospel and founded new churches, laying the foundations that were necessary to see the church succeed.

They utilized the evangelistic ministry to bring in the lost by preaching the good news of the gospel of Jesus Christ. Additionally, planting a new church required a prophetic orientation, so that the apostles could discern the spiritual needs of that community. Once the churches were formed, they handled problems as they arose and appointed local elders to care for the new church opening the way for the pastoral and teaching ministries.

Apostles, prophets and evangelists are essential in the early days of a church plant. Apostles lay foundations and prophets break through spiritual strongholds. Evangelists bring in the unsaved and help a new church reach out to their new community. Later, pastors and teachers are involved in the long term care and nurture of the church as it grows. Pastors help provide a place of safety and comfort to the people, and teachers help bring the saints to maturity.

The New Testament documents the flurry of churches being planted throughout the known world. In fact, it reads like a church planting manual:

Acts 2:42 Birth of the modern church
(church planted in Jerusalem)

Acts 8:14 Planting of Samaria church

Acts 9:20 Church in Damascus

Acts 9:31 Church in Judea

Acts 13:44 Whole city gathers to hear the Word of the Lord

Virtually all the great evangelistic challenges of the New Testament are calls to plant churches. This is why a leading missiologist like Peter Wagner says, "Planting new churches is the most effective evangelistic methodology known under heaven."[2]

Planting churches in the New Testament pattern requires a church-multiplying movement that involves the fivefold ministry functioning in all of its power and anointing. The fivefold ministry will never be fully developed unless fivefold ministers are released into church planting as they multiply themselves.

Impact of apostles on church planting

The apostles especially have an important role to play in planting churches because they are the establishers and architects. Their essential call is to plant new churches as they reflect the intent of their sender, Jesus Christ. While they do not necessarily plant all of the church plants, it is important for them to obtain experience in church planting before they are declared apostles. They need to know what others will go through. Because they have already done it, they have faith to see it happen again and train others.

When you are around an apostolic person, faith overflows and feeds into you and causes you to believe that you can accomplish what God is telling you to do. An apostle is always thinking about expansion, planting new churches, expanding what already is.

Someone with a pastoral anointing will have a hard time seeing the need to plant a church. He will be satisfied to pastor a church for many years without starting another one. It takes someone with an apostolic anointing to jump start a pastor into realizing he can send his worship leader, youth leader or other church leader out to start another church. Pastors need apostolic oversight to keep their vision stirred for the lost.

An apostle will think in terms of sending out the best to get the job done while a pastor many times will want to hold the best to keep his church working properly. Pastors need the apostolic gift to help them think outside the box and dream.

Sam, the senior pastor of a mega church in my area, is such a pastor who thinks outside the box. He says, "God's dream is that none should perish. Knowing the dream of the Lord requires that we continue to plant many more churches. We cannot be content with the status quo. In fact if we are content with the status quo, many more people will enter a Christless eternity and the kingdom will not advance, and that is the worst case scenario there is."

The apostolic gift will activate and impart spiritual gifts

Paul anticipated that Timothy would need to act on what he had learned.

Timothy, my son, I give you this instruction...according to the prophecies previously made concerning you, that by them you may wage the good warfare.... [3]

Paul's apostolic gift was used in his relationship with Timothy to fulfill his God-given destiny. He understood the tactics of the enemy and encouraged Timothy to press through. Timothy was used tremendously by the Holy Spirit in the early church plants. We can't just sit on what we have heard. We need to do something with those words. Apostolic leaders encourage their people to activate their gifts.

The apostolic gift brings unity in a region

When a new church plant was begun in Edmonton, Canada, one of our church's apostolic leaders met with other pastors in the area and introduced them to the new church planter who was starting to build a new church in the community. They expressed their desire to work together, rather than compete with one another. In this way, they demonstrated to the other churches in the region that they desired to be accountable to see the kingdom built in the community.

Existing pastors who have been laboring for years in a community and have invested their lives in the community often do not welcome a new upstart church if they do not understand where they are coming from. When the existing churches observe that the new plant has spiritual protection and accountability from a larger apostolic source, it brings security and encourages open dialog and relationship.

The apostolic gift helps church planters avoid burnout

There are "pioneer" church planters and "ranchers." The pioneer church planters like to go in and carve out a new church and then move on after a year or so. The apostolic leaders help to ensure that other leaders are raised up to take over when the pioneer planter is ready to move again.

Otherwise the pioneer church planter becomes burned out if he has to stay and nurture the church for a long period of time. In some cases, because of his constant need to pioneer something new, a pioneer planter may unintentionally begin to tear down what he has previously built, just so he can rebuild.

A "rancher" church planter is one who is content to clear new land and stay for awhile. He may clear adjoining land eventually, but he is there to stay and raise his family and grow bigger. If he would be required to move on, he would burn out because it is not in his nature to continually start new churches. His desire is to establish roots, dig deeply into the fabric of the community and stand against the enemy's tactics.

Apostolic leaders sense and discern what each leader needs and helps each one to build accordingly. If a church planter does not understand the difference between these two dynamics, he will be frustrated over a period of time and may conclude that he is not cut out for church leadership when, in fact, he is just misplaced.

Apostolic/prophetic warfare

The church is built upon the foundation of the apostle and prophets (Ephesians 2:20). This can be no more true than in church planting. Apostolic/prophetic teams are especially helpful in identifying spiritual strongholds in the new area and helping church planters break through the spiritual darkness in their city. Prophetic prayer teams can come in and stir up the spiritual cobwebs of a community tearing down influences that hinder a plant from moving forward.

Sometimes I encourage one of our new church planters to have a prophetic team come in and pray over the region. Teams like this are quite effective as they come in and set up their spiritual antenna, picking up the weaknesses and strengths of the area. Ministry focus can be determined more effectively when this happens.

Teachers lay groundwork

As the new plant begins to grow, it is important to have gifted teachers to come in on a regular basis to lay a firm foundation. Weekend teaching sessions can easily be introduced, momentum builds and new Christians become hungry for the Word of the Lord. This is an excellent time to use developing teachers because they can lay basic, foundational truths.

It also is a time where long-lasting relationships can be developed over a period of time. In one particular new church plant, we had fivefold teachers come in who made a powerful impression on the new Christians in that church. And while these teachers do not come around as often now, they are clearly remembered as having a tremendous impact on the lives of these new believers.

Conclusion

As all of the gifted fivefold ministers are released into their God-given callings in church planting, each adds vital parts to the whole picture. The apostles spot other apostles and train them, the prophets train other prophets, and pastors, teachers and evangelists do the same. This pattern in church planting not only helps jump-start new churches, it also benefits existing churches because the fivefold ministers reach maturity with their practical, hands-on training.

CHAPTER 16

Build Lasting Relationships

Practical tips for relationships between church leaders and fivefold ministers

The needs of the fivefold ministers and how church leaders should respond to these needs is vitally important. Most of the problems in dealing with fivefold translocal ministers center around unmet expectations. What is the pastor expecting when he invites a fivefold minister to his church, and what is a fivefold minister expecting when a pastor invites him in?

A fivefold minister should know that his needs are going to be taken care of. A pastor should be comfortable that the fivefold minister is going to help him build what the Holy Spirit is building. The pastor should know how to communicate his expectations to the fivefold minister. The result of this understanding is fruitful ministry with long-lasting results for both!

Communication is key. Pastor, remember to return e-mails and phone calls. This may seem basic, but when you have 20 different appointments on your schedule in the next few days, and forget to return e-mails and phone calls to your fivefold minister, you are devaluing him.

The fivefold minister will minister with a sense that he has fulfilled the purposes of God in that congregation, while at the same time, feel honored and valued by the pastor. They know the Lord was in the experience and will remain open to what He has in the future as they continue to build a relationship.

Building through an ongoing relationship is an effective building process. Yet, far too many fivefold ministers are under-utilized, ministering on a onetime basis rather than building a lasting relationship with a congregation. There may be a wonderful anointing, but often, the fruit is not lasting and because it is a one time occurrence it becomes a flash in the pan. When the fivefold minister is deprived of an ongoing relationship with the local church body, he is deprived of an opportunity to build long-lasting fruit—fruit that will not only remain but also bear more fruit.

Numerous times, I have heard pastors remark about a visiting fivefold minister, "I will not have him back again." After ministering the second time at his church, one pastor admitted, "You are only the second person that we have ever invited back for the second time." He had bad experiences with previous fivefold ministers which made him understandably cautious. I believe the Lord wants to bring some adjustment and correction so that lasting fruit is evident and there is more effective ministry occurring.

I have been a local elder, a senior elder and a fivefold minister. I have experienced times when the relationship between the fivefold ministry and local church flowed really well. Other times, some minor adjustments would have made things flow more smoothly in order to facilitate more effective long-term ministry.

I received a call one day from a fivefold minister who had just served at one of the local churches I oversee. He stressed that he was not offended in any way, but just wanted to encourage me to do some training in the church on how to handle visiting ministers! I immediately knew what he was talking about because I recalled seeing him leave the church building that Sunday morning after speaking. He was crawling into the back seat of a tiny compact car, and because he was a fairly sizeable man, I remembered thinking that using a larger car to take him to the airport would have been much more comfortable.

He went on to tell me the rest of the story. As they were driving out of the parking lot, the minister even mentioned to the senior leader that it would be nice if they had a larger car to go to the airport. The driver cheerfully responded, "When in Rome, do as the Romans do." However, they were following a large sport utility vehicle that was being driven by one of the leaders of the church. Apparently, not every "Roman" drove a compact car! They could have easily found someone with a larger vehicle for the long drive to the airport.

To make matters worse, on the way to the airport, they experienced car trouble. The air conditioner failed and the car began to overheat. Although they made it, there was a question as to whether they would get there on time. While we have all had car trouble at one time or another, a quick decision to take a better car to the airport would have resulted in a much less stressful experience for the minister.

In addition, no one at the church had communicated whether the minister would receive an offering for his service or whether a check would be forthcoming in the mail. Or, was he donating his time and receiving nothing more that a "thank you" and "bless you for ministering to us this morning" from the church?

While all of us have ministered at times as a labor of love, and we may need to do that when there is a legitimate need, the fivefold translocal ministers also have bills to pay. Their cars get old, their children grow out of clothes and they even stop fasting at times to eat! God does not supernaturally grow finances on a tree in their back yard. They work and earn their financial support through their ministry.

Let's learn together how to relate to the fivefold ministers when we invite them to our small group or church. Some of the following items may seem elementary, but sometimes it is the elementary things that are forgotten and when something is forgotten, it almost always has a negative result.

1. The worker deserves his wages

When you are inviting a minister to speak at your church or small group, find out if there is a fee he is expecting to receive. A few ministers have a set fee they normally charge, but it is most customary to receive love offerings or honorariums. If they have a set fee, you can decide right away whether you wish to have them come and minister. It is always safe to ask what they are expecting or what they have been accustomed to. Fivefold ministers should be paid for their services. The Bible is very clear that you should "...not muzzle the ox while it is treading out the grain," and "the worker deserves his wages" (1 Timothy 5:18).

If the fivefold minister does not have a set fee, then payment for his services can be handled one of the following ways: honorarium, love offering or love offering plus an honorarium. Each church has its own custom, but I would venture to say that many churches are probably a little behind in the amount that they think of giving a fivefold person for ministering. While in years past it may have been acceptable to give $300 every time a fivefold minister spoke, it would be very hard to make a living on just ministering at $300 per speaking engagement unless he is speaking four to five times a week. If it is a small group that he is ministering at, obviously this figure would be lower, but if it is an average size congregation, then a larger amount is expected.

I recommend that you give the minister a love offering plus an honorarium, especially if he is supporting a ministry. That gives the Lord the opportunity to bless the individual according to current needs and those needs for which he is believing God. It also gives the congregation the freedom to respond to the Holy Spirit without putting pressure on the finances of the local church. Notice, I said *love offering plus honorarium*. I believe a local church has the responsibility to "pay for services rendered." I am more than willing to pay for any other service that I receive, so I should be so much more willing to pay for services in the kingdom. I am blessing another one of God's children.

Do not be afraid to give too much in the way of financial blessing. This individual is a minister of the Lord to whom you have just entrusted the preaching of the Word and the ministry of the Holy Spirit to your small group or congregation. Certainly, you should be able to trust him that if you gave him "too much" he will pass it on to others in need. I know of individuals who, under the direction of the Holy Spirit, gave their entire honorarium away as soon as they received it because they saw a need right there within the body in which they were ministering. We must trust these workers with finances if we are going to trust them to deliver to us true riches. There still is a poverty type mentality in many churches that needs to be broken. While this is not true in many churches, it is in some, and if it is in yours, I encourage you to break it by giving above what has been normal for you.

An important principle to remember is this: be generous. God's kingdom is not one of stinginess. It is a kingdom of blessing. If the speaker has really blessed the people in your church, receive a love offering and allow the Holy Spirit to bless the individual as He wants to. If you are afraid to do that, check your heart. Are you concerned that it would take money away from other offerings? If so, you are communicating to your people that God will not supply your needs. It is thinking that once God provides, we should hold on to it because He may not provide again. That spirit alone will hinder the release of finances in your congregation.

I have heard people say that Paul is talking about *respect* when he said, "The elders who direct the affairs of the church well are worthy of double honor, especially those whose work is preaching and teaching" (1 Timothy 5:17). While it is true that we need to respect those who minister the Word, my perception of this scripture is that Paul is referring here to *finances*. Verse 18 goes on to say that a "worker deserves his wages."

When you go to the garage to pick up your repaired car, you do not tell the mechanic, "I respect you; in fact I doubly respect you."

His response is sure to be, "That's great that you respect me. Here is your bill. Please pay it immediately."

To bring matters into perspective, imagine this scenario. If we give between $150 to $250 to a minister who spent eight to ten hours in prayer and preparation for a ministry event and add the hours for travel and ministry time, we end up giving him less than $10 an hour. In the United States, we pay a mechanic $55 to $75 an hour to repair our cars! This seems a little out of balance to me. Anytime we invest into a kingdom individual, we are investing into the kingdom. The kingdom of God pays dividends that are comparable to none. As we invest into God's people, the Lord invests in us.

An exception to this principle might be that I do not pay for training someone in the early stages of development in the local church. If I am giving someone the opportunity to learn by exercising his gift, I usually do not give him an honorarium. There may come a time, sometime during the training, that I begin to bless him financially for ministering. Again, the key here is expectation. I clearly tell him that I am training him and giving him an opportunity, but it is part of his training. He will not be paid for it other than being blessed by this opportunity to serve.

However you decide to handle it, either by honorarium, love offering or a combination of the two, communicate to the individual what he should expect. Feel free to ask him if he has a preference. Don't be afraid to talk to him about money. There is nothing sacred or unholy about finances. They are a reality of life. Ask him, "To whom should the check be made out?" or in the case of a love offering, "Do you want cash?" (In the USA, remember that if the check or cash is over $600 and is made out to the individual rather than a ministry, you will need to send him an IRS 1099 form at the end of the year for income tax purposes. For accounting purposes, it is always better to write the check out to the ministry he represents.)

While ministering, I have been in small churches and received five hundred dollars and in large churches and received a hundred dollars. I have been in medium-size churches where I have received much more. Size is not the indicator of blessing.

Some of the aspects that influence our thinking about giving come from our backgrounds. Certain denominations may consistently give more or less than others. Some of that is the value that is placed on the mantle a minister carries. It often involves their understanding of finances and how ministers should be supported. We are all products of what we have been exposed to, and our values reflect that. We should ask ourselves, "Do our values reflect God's values of giving or do they reflect a certain denomination's values?"

A true kingdom-building fivefold translocal minister is not in it for the money. He ministers because he has sensed that the Lord asked him to. He is not looking at the money; he is looking to obey the Lord. A fivefold minister sees a much larger picture. There are places that the Lord asks him to go where, due to the economics of the church or the area, he needs to provide for his own expenses. I have done this while traveling both nationally and internationally. A minister does this willingly because he knows he is a servant of the Lord and desires to see God's kingdom advanced. A fivefold minister is looking to the Lord to supply his needs. He expects that the Lord will meet those needs from those who have abundance to help supply for him to go to those who have a great need (2 Corinthians 8:13-15).

2. Travel expenses

Whether the minister is flying or driving, there are travel expenses that need to be covered. Ask the individual how he wants it to be handled. Does he want a separate check? Or, can the amount be included on the honorarium check? Who should the check(s) be made out to? Do they need the travel expenses before they arrive to cover the costs of airline tickets? Or, can they wait until after the engagement to receive reimbursement? Do they wish to purchase the ticket and get reimbursed, or would they prefer you to buy the ticket and send it to them? For those who are frequent flyers, there is usually an airline that they favor for a variety of reasons. Try to honor special requests when possible. By asking these kinds of questions, you are letting them know that you value them and that their needs are important to you.

Again, the key question is, "What does he expect?" Either provide transportation costs or give a large enough honorarium or love offering to offset the transportation expenses, even if there is a relatively short travel distance.

Let's get practical. If he drives one hundred miles to the place of ministry and one hundred miles home, that is a two hundred mile round-trip. Most travel distances are much farther. If he receives the current amount allowed by the U.S. government at the time of this writing (56.5 cents per mile), the total is more than a hundred dollars for mileage reimbursement. If he receives a few hundred dollars for an honorarium, remember that it cost him more than a hundred dollars to travel there. When you figure in his preparation and ministry time (let's say ten hours to pray and prepare), payment for his ministry starts to equate to somewhere between eight to ten dollars per hour. My teenage son was paid that much several years ago for sweeping floors in a cabinet shop. While these figures may differ from what is customary for you, I am sure you understand the concept. As a pastor, think through things practically.

We must make the distinction about what it costs for travel and how much we're paying for ministry. Sometimes it is easier to do this if we give two checks, one for expenses and one for ministering. If we put them both together it looks like we are giving more to them for their ministry then we actually are. Again, my point here is that ministers need to be reimbursed for their expenses and also for their ministry. They are not in it for the money, but they do have legitimate expenses that are going to be covered, either by you, which is proper, or out of their own pockets. Try to place yourself in their shoes as you compute their financial reimbursement.

3. Lodging Arrangements

Ask in advance if the minister has a preference for lodging. Does he want to stay in a motel or would he prefer to stay in the home of someone from the fellowship? There is not a right or wrong to this; it is purely a preference. Some ministers desire to stay in the home of someone from the fellowship or perhaps even with the local senior leader. Others dislike the inconvenience of sharing bathrooms with family members and are very uncomfortable with this type of arrangement.

Some homes are laid out in such a way that it is almost like being in a motel—the minister has his own bathroom and does not feel like he is intruding on the hosting family. Ask him what his values are. One of my personal values is that I will not be alone with another woman other than my wife. I do not want to be left alone in the house with just the wife if her husband needs to go to work or to a meeting in the morning.

If I'm staying in a home, I like to know what the sleeping arrangements are. I've slept in many different places. I've slept in the son's bedroom on the top bunk with "glow in the dark stars" just above my head. I've slept in the daughter's bedroom with the dolls and a mound of stuffed animals I had to move off the bed so I could crawl in. There is nothing wrong with any of these arrangements. In fact, I believe there is a blessing in store for the young child who is willing to give up his or her room for the visiting minister. Usually it depends upon how close a relationship I have with the family. If I have no relationship, or I'm just beginning to build a relationship, it feels as if I'm intruding on the family to sleep in one of the children's bedrooms, and it can feel quite uncomfortable. If I already have an established relationship with the family, then I am very comfortable with this style arrangement. In fact, I look forward to this relationship-building time.

Some time ago, I was going to speak at a church where they informed me of arrangements for me to stay with two single women.

I responded that I preferred a motel even if I had to personally pay for it. They quickly assured me that the women in whose home I would be staying were "older women." To me, that didn't matter. A story like that repeated through the "grapevine" can easily develop into a rumor that places me in a house alone with two women, and it will not include the fact that they are grandmothers! They were very gracious and found another place for me to stay.

Here are some things to be mindful of when considering the minister's lodging:

Is there a place to pray freely?

Does he have his own bathroom?

Is there a desk and chair for study?

Is there wifi for correspondance and social media?

Can he charge meals to the room?

Be careful of "Bed and Breakfast" establishments since most are geared toward vacationers. Think of creating a work environment for the speaker. I stayed in a Bed and Breakfast one time and shared the bathroom with a young couple in the adjacent room who were celebrating their one year wedding anniversary. The whole environment was a bit uncomfortable.

We really must take into consideration the different dynamics to which we subject ministers. Sometimes it is just because we do not put enough thought into where we are placing them. In my opinion, another lodging location to avoid is a cabin in the woods. I have had some interesting experiences in rustic cabins in the woods, and while they are funny now, they were not while I was experiencing them!

Most speakers work with mobile devices and maintain contact with their personal intercessors and social media. Try to make sure they have the opportunity to do that. They need places where they can pray and study. This is not a vacation for them. It is work. Provide a place where they can work properly. They need an environment where they can study, get alone with God, receive from Him and be refreshed.

4. Meal Plans

The fourth area to consider is food. If the minister is only there for a Sunday morning, take him to lunch. Mealtime is an excellent time to discuss issues relating to leadership, the Word that was spoken and other things happening in the body of Christ. The translocal minister is usually someone who is traveling quite a bit, so he is exposed to things that local leadership would not normally be exposed to. This is a great time to get outside input and fresh perspective on what is happening in the body of Christ at large.

If you cannot personally take the guest minister to lunch, have another key leader do it, especially one with a similar gift. For example, if the fivefold minister is an evangelist, send an evangelist-leader from your church. This indicates to your leader that he is of value and worth by allowing him to get some quality one-on-one time with the equipping minister.

As a fivefold minister, I have personally had the opportunity to communicate valuable principles to key leaders in a restaurant over lunch. Sometimes a visiting minister can impart things into leaders that the senior leader has not been able to. I can encourage teamwork, help them see things from a different perspective, and encourage them to walk through difficult situations. It is often helpful to have someone from the outside speak into existing situations or difficulties.

If the fivefold minister is ministering for more than one meeting, here are some different food options to consider:

If he is there in the morning, does he want breakfast? Some are not big breakfast fans while others are used to starting their day with a full breakfast.

If he is there in the evening, would he rather eat before or after ministering? Regardless of whether it is before or after keep in mind what he would like to eat.

Be sensitive to how late you keep him up as he may want to pray and get a fresh sense of what the Lord is saying for the next service.

Does he have food preferences, likes or dislikes? Some people love Chinese food, and others don't. Ask if there is a specific kind of food he would like.

Does he like fresh fruit? Would he like some fruit in his room? It is always nice to have some bottled water and a few snacks in the room for when he returns from ministry. You are taking care of his needs so that he can be focused on what the Lord is saying to the church.

If he is staying in a hotel or motel and is arriving without you being there, make sure the room is reserved in his name, but billed to you.

After he is checked in, call and ask if everything is satisfactory in the room. Make sure that the room wasn't charged to him. Inform him of a restaurant on the premises and whether he can charge food to the room.

All these things may seem basic, but they are important since they communicate that you care. Clear communication will help the fivefold minister to be more effective in ministering to your congregation or small group.

5. Ministry Needs

You should take into consideration if the fivefold minister has any special needs for ministry. Does he need a white board? Does he use PowerPoint or videos for illustration?

Does the minister need copies of handouts printed for distribution? Does he have a microphone preference? Would he rather use a hand-held, lapel microphone or ear mount? Does he need to preach from the platform? Are there areas in the room that cause feedback in the microphones? These are all things better communicated beforehand then experienced mid service.

Are there any specific worship songs that would be effective in helping to prepare the hearts of the people for his ministry? Is he planning a ministry time after the preaching? If so, does he need prayer counselors, ushers to set up ministry lines or other ministers to help assist in ministry? Let him know if you have trained counselors available. Communicate how you normally do ministry so that he knows what the people are accustomed to. What type of response is he anticipating? Does he want the worship team back for the ministry time or does he prefer it to be quiet? Or would he prefer just a keyboard? Is he anticipating moving prophetically? Will he minister prophetically over individuals? If so, is there a recording device available to record the personal prophesies?

As a pastor, I would want recording happening for the entire service, capturing everything that is taking place. More than once, the Lord released a prophetic word and afterwards the sound man said that he did not capture it because he had not yet started recording the service. That report is always met with disappointment.

Who does the fivefold minister turn the meeting back to when he is finished ministering? Does he end the service with ministry time, or does he turn it back to the pastor? If someone other than the pastor is moderating, does it go back to the moderator or the pastor?

Ask him if he would like to receive a copy of the message. Some ministers find it helpful to listen to the message again to critique themselves or provide the message for someone else to listen to.

If you were planning to receive a love offering after the message, how will it mesh with the ministry time? Some pastors ask the fivefold minister to give a five-minute testimony about his ministry before he preaches. This way the pastor receives a love offering for him before he gives his message, opening the door for a time of prayer ministry at the end of the service. If at all possible it is always better to receive the love offering after he ministers. People's hearts are open to the Lord and can respond to the voice of the Lord more adequately after he ministers. If you receive the offering before, most people will give something out of obligation but not a real sense of sowing into the individual. Are there other announcements that need to be given before the close of the service? All of this is helpful to the minister so that he can be sensitive about how the Holy Spirit is leading and what the pastor has planned to happen at the end of the service. If this is shared before the service begins, it helps provide a divine flow at the end.

6. Bringing clarity to the message

In light of the Word that was preached, we should be open to any corrections or adjustments that are necessary. Any seasoned qualified fivefold minister, who has the kingdom of God in his heart, is there to help you build what the Holy Spirit is building. If he says something that needs to be corrected or adjusted for your fellowship, do it right away at the end of the service, if possible. It will be contained at that moment and clarified, leaving no doubts. If something is said that needs to be corrected but is done at a later date, you will not be able to completely correct it. Once people leave it is almost impossible to follow-up with everyone that was in attendance. As a leader you need to be aware that your people will always watch you to see how you are responding with "nonverbals" while another minister is ministering. If the minister says something challenging, eyes will look to the leader, does he agree or disagree, is he receiving or not receiving what is being said. So, as the leader, make sure that you are paying attention to what is being ministered so that you can receive all that is being said but also so that you do not hinder anyone else from receiving as well.

Before I minister, I always ask the leader to feel free to bring clarity if I say something that is contrary to what he is ministering in his church. For example, if I refer to my understanding of a woman's role in fivefold ministry, and the church believes differently, the leader needs to bring clarity to what was communicated. He should feel free to say something like, "I appreciate what Ron had to share this morning, but I want to bring clarity to what he said about women in fivefold ministry. We believe that the Lord has instructed us such and such in this matter." As a fivefold minister, I will not be offended with this adjustment.

In the case of a new concept or thought, the leader could say, "I am not sure about what Ron shared today. I am going to study the scriptures and encourage you to do likewise and I'll have a response for you at a later date." If, as the leader, you believe a fivefold minister shares something clearly wrong, bring adjustment immediately at the close of the service: "We do not agree with (the specific issue) spoken here and we will be in dialogue with Ron about it at lunch, but we wanted to bring clarity to that right away." This case scenario would rarely happen, but you need to be prepared if it does. If you clearly trust the individual, let him know you trust him and tell him, "I give you complete freedom and liberty in the Spirit today to minister all that is on your heart." If you want to draw parameters, do so before the fivefold minister speaks. "Our policy here is that all prophetic words be run by one of the leaders before it is spoken publicly." Any policies or methods of ministry are important to communicate *before* ministry happens to avoid awkwardness and embarrassment for everyone.

Remember, as a church leader, you have spiritual responsibility and authority for the field or sphere that the Lord has given you, namely the church that he is ministering in. He knows that he is in your field, and if he doesn't, it is better that he find out before he ministers than after. Don't be afraid to exercise the authority the Lord has given you for that field. Do it with grace and in a way that can easily be received, but do it. You have invited a fivefold translocal minister into your "field," and he needs to honor the leadership of that field. As the God-ordained leader of the fellowship you should, along with your team, exercise good, godly government and leadership.

7. Reimbursement

As was mentioned before, at the end of the speaking engagement, communicate again with the minister about payment for his services. Make sure you know who the check should be made out to, especially if you are able to give him a check immediately. If you're going to mail a check, let him know when he can expect to receive it. Many fivefold traveling ministers use the finances they receive today to pay for an upcoming trip. They may need to receive their funds as soon as possible. Also, if they know that it will take a week to receive the check, they can plan for it. Once they leave, it is easy to remember the wonderful ministry time but forget to mail the check. Clearly communicate, so that they know what to expect. On more than one occasion I have ministered at a church where they said they would send the check, but I waited and waited. Sometimes it came after a number of weeks; sometimes it was completely forgotten. If I know when to expect it, it becomes much easier to approach the subject after the expected arrival time with a grace filled e-mail or phone call. "Hi, I was just checking on the check that you were going to mail. I haven't received it and I was just letting you know in case there was a problem with the mail or if it was an oversight." When I know what and when to expect it, all the concern over it is taken away.

8. Debriefing

The process of debriefing is extremely important. As soon as possible, talk to the fivefold minister and find out what he was sensing while he was ministering. Sometimes people from the "outside" are able to sense a whole lot more than people from the "inside." That is why it is so important to get a sense of what he was feeling during his time of ministry. Did he find the people receptive? Did he sense a freedom to minister? Was there anything he sensed about your leadership? How can you be a more effective leader? How about worship? Was it releasing and freeing and did he sense people responding?

An outside fivefold minister may be able to pick up on something that you are unable to sense in-house. Sometimes the fivefold minister may have a prophetic sense about an individual because he stands out. By asking for input, you are getting an insight into what is emanating from the people of the congregation. The fivefold minister may sense a specific area of oppression that needs to be broken or something that you should be focusing on in the next few months. Take his insights very seriously, but also remember, we have all had services when things did not flow well. Consequently, always take the fivefold minister's input before the Lord for adjustment.

An exceptional service with a fivefold minister does not mean the church will flourish, and a horrible experience will not cause a church to fail. The truth is that sometimes everything flows extremely well during ministry and the next time, no matter how hard we try to stay sensitive to the Spirit's leading, it just doesn't seem to go right. Be aware that God's grace is there to cover.

Make sure that after you have received all that the fivefold minister has to give to you, *you* minister to *him*. Affirm him. He is a servant of the Lord, a fellow soldier, and under the attack of the enemy. If he really ministered to you and your congregation, tell him. Avoid flattering words like, "awesome message," "tremendous ministry," "that was really wild!" These words are not quantifiable and can easily be misunderstood. Use descriptive words like, "I really felt you ministered the heart of the Lord this morning. What you shared today is exactly what we need as a congregation to move forward in the next step that the Lord has for us." Or, "I could really sense the anointing this morning. The presence of God was tangible today. Thank you for investing in us today. We so appreciate your willingness to come and give of your time and expertise."

Follow up

If there is a need for you to give input to the fivefold minister, now is the time to do it. This is probably a little more difficult to do, but necessary. If you have constructive input, say something like:

"I think you would be more effective in your ministry if you would...."

"When you said..., it put up walls that hindered the true Word of the Lord from being heard today."

"In the future you might want to consider...."

I know of one situation where the guest fivefold minister stopped in the middle of his message and said, "You know what, we need to take an offering for the ministry in which I am involved." He looked at the pastor, "Is that okay?" Before the pastor could answer he went on to say, "Yes, that feels right, let's take an offering." And he proceeded to call the ushers forward to receive an offering for himself. Undoubtedly, there was the need for some constructive criticism to take place with that fivefold minister afterwards!

Remember that you are in ministry together. You want to learn from his experience and you want to share with him from yours. It is a "give and take"—one in which everybody can win! A leader can be blessed by how the Lord ministers through the fivefold minister and the fivefold minister will be blessed by the way the leader honors and takes care of him.

As the leader of the church, you are representing Jesus to the church. If both the church leader and fivefold minister keep that in mind, with a servant's heart, ministry will be productive and have a lasting effect, and that is a win–win situation!

Let's risk it!

Yes, Jesus took a risk in determining that we are the ones to extend the kingdom of God. He empowered us to be involved in the lives of people, conforming them to the image of God. He gave gifts to us to help us in that process. But we will have to take a risk to see them released.

I encourage you to take a risk today and begin to establish effective fivefold ministry in your fellowship. If you are a budding apostle, prophet, evangelist, pastor or teacher, I urge you to take a risk and step out in faith. Come alongside the leadership team of your local church and its vision and support that church until you see the vision succeed. As we work together, I believe the vision of the Lord's Bride, working together in unity, can become a reality.

Enjoy the adventure!

Fivefold Ministry Seminar: We receive many requests for training fivefold ministers within the local church. In response, we offer live training on Fivefold Ministry through a Fivefold Seminar that you can host at your own church. For information on hosting a seminar, check out our web site at www.dcfi.org.

Fivefold ministry

Apostle, apostolic AUTHORITY
Fatherly authority
Mobilizes gifts and resources for outreach
Keeps us founded on Christ
Keeps a vision for God's purposes before us
Imparts callings, gifts
Deep concern for unity in body of Christ
Some apostles lay foundations for new congregations
Some apostles help to set things in order, in existing churches

Prophet, prophetic REVELATION
Thrust us forward in our vision
Activates our spiritual gifts
Calls us to holiness and righteousness
Keeps us alert to the manifest presence of Christ
Imparts a spirit of prayer and intercession
Speaks words with creative power to change lives
Has a heart to edify, comfort, exhort
Lays foundations in individuals, ministries upon Christ
Imparts power and gifts for ministry

Evangelist, evangelistic RESPONSE
Helps people to understand and respond to the basic biblical message of
        salvation, cleansing, baptism, filling of Spirit, gifts of Spirit
Causes non-believers to find salvation and forgiveness
Motivates believers to share the gospel with others
Stirs people to action, respond to God
Breaks bondages of excuses, inactivity, indecisiveness, laziness
Brings conviction of sins
Helps people to receive Christ and become established in a local congregation

Pastor, pastoral NURTURE
Speaks in a way that brings security and acceptance
Draws people together in Christ, gathering into body
Breaks bondages of independence, isolation, insecurity
Supernatural drawing to oneself for counsel and love
Feels with people; concerned from their point of view

Becomes intimately involved with his congregation, small group, class
Feeds and leads one's people what is good for growth

Teacher, teaching TRUTH
Maintains accuracy in handling God's Word
Enables us to understand God's truth
Sets people free from deception and error
Unfolding practical life-style that fits with sound doctrine
Helps people to live by principles, not circumstances

To what extent are these anointings evident in me?

	Strong	Some	Little	None
Apostolic	5	3	1	0
Prophetic	5	3	1	0
Teaching	5	3	1	0
Pastoral	5	3	1	0
Evangelistic	5	3	1	0

Name_____Date_____

Christ in you (all), the hope of glory!

Several concepts used in developing this survey were derived from *the book Complete Wineskin*, by Harold Eberle.

Used by permission of Teaching The Word Ministries, © February 1993, One Mayfield Drive, Leola, PA 17540, Email: mail@ttwm.org, Web site: www.ttwm.org

Notes

Chapter 1

1. Luke 24:49
2. Philip Schaff, *History of the Christian Church, Vol. 1, Apostolic Christianity: A.D. 1-100* (Grand Rapids: Eerdmans, 1910), pp. 381-2, 329-330.
3. Hebrews 10:34

Chapter 2

1. Edited by Matthew D. Green, *Understanding the Fivefold Ministry*, "Beyond Novelty to Substance," Jack Hayford, (Florida: Charisma House, 2005), p.xi
2. Ibid., "The Leadershift," Doug Beacham

Chapter 3

1. Vinson Synan, Ph.D., Regent University School of Divinity, *"Apostolic Practice,"* Encounter: Journal for Pentecostal Ministry, Winter 2005 (Vol. 2, No. 1)

Chapter 4

1. Galatians 1:10
2. Ephesians 4:13
3. Luke 16:10
4. Mark 4:28
5. Acts 13:1
6. Acts 15:2, 30-35, 40-41
7. Galatians 1:1, 8-9; Galatians 2:1-2,7-8

Chapter 5

1. Ephesians 4:13
2. Dr. Bill Hamon: Restoring the Fivefold Ministry, *The 700 Club*, April 23, 2004

Chapter 6

1. Hebrews 3:1-2
2. Luke 6:12; Acts 1:15; 4:33; Revelation 21:14
3. Romans 16:7; Ephesians 4; 1 Corinthians 12:28; 1 Corinthians 4:6, 9; 1 Timothy 1:1
4. John 15:20b
5. Galatians 4:14
6. Acts 18:11
7. Acts 19:8-10
8. Acts 28:31
9. 1 Timothy 1:3
10. 2 Timothy 4:21
11. Titus 1:5
12. Titus 3:12
13. Ephesians 4:11-13
14. 1 Corinthians 3:10
15. Ephesians 4:11; 1 Corinthians 12:28; 1 Corinthians 12:29
16. *Your Spiritual Gifts Can Help Your Church Grow,* Peter Wagner, (Ventura, CA: Gospel Light, 2005)
17. Edited by Matthew D. Green, *Understanding the Fivefold Ministry*, "The Doc Responds," Peter Wagner, (Florida: Charisma House, 2005), p.31
18. Romans 1:1
19. Acts 13:1-4
20. Romans 15:20
21. Romans 11:13
22. Galatians 2:8
23. 2 Corinthians 11:13-15; Revelation 2:2
24. Acts 14:21-23
25. Galatians 1:18-22
26. Galatians 1:1
27. 1 Thessalonians 1:1
28. 1 Corinthians 3:5-15
29. 2 Corinthians 10:13-18
30. 1 Timothy 1:1-4; Titus 1:5
31. 1 Corinthians 9:1-2
32. 2 Corinthians 12:12
33. 1 Corinthians 9:1-2; 1 Corinthians 15:9; Acts 13:1; 2 Timothy 1:11
34. 1 Timothy 3:2-7
35. Matthew 20:26-28
36. Philippians 2:5-8
37. 1 Corinthians 4:15-21
38. John 3:30
39. Acts 13:13
40. 1 Corinthians 4:9-13; 2 Corinthians 6:3-10
41. Ephesians 2:19-22
42. 1 Corinthians 12:28-29

Chapter 7

1. Hebrews 1:2; Hebrews 2:1-4
2. 1 John 2:20
3. Edited by Matthew D. Green, *Understanding the Fivefold Ministry*, "Speaking God's Thoughts," Ernest Gentile, (Florida: Charisma House, 2005), p.73
4. Titus 1:6-9
5. Acts 15:32
6. Acts 21:10-11
7. Acts 21:10-14
8. 1 Corinthians 13:9
9. Matthew 7:15-23; Titus 3:9-11

Chapter 8

[1] 1 John 14:6
[2] Jared C. Wilson, *The Prodigal Church: A Gentle Manifesto against the Status Quo* (Wheaton, IL, Crossway, 2015), p. 39
[3] 1 Peter 4:10 (NKJV)
[4] Matthew 10:1-20
[5] Acts 21:8
[6] Acts 6:5
[7] 2 Timothy 2:15
[8] Acts 8:6,13
[9] Acts 8:35
[10] Acts 8:37
[11] Ephesians 4:13
[12] 2 Timothy 4:5; 1 Thessalonians 3:2

Chapter 9

[1] Charles Simpson, *The Challenge to Care, A Fresh Look at Pastors and Lay Leaders Relate to People of God,* (Ann Arbor, Michigan: Servant Publications, 1986)
[2] An excellent book called *Hearing God 30 Different Ways* by Larry Kreider (Lititz, Pennsylvania: House to House Publications, 2005) is available at our network of churches website: www.dcfi.org
[3] John 10:10-15
[4] Romans 12

Chapter 10

[1] Edited by Matthew D. Green, *Understanding the Fivefold Ministry,* "Itching Ears," R.T. Kendall, (Florida: Charisma House, 2005), p.153, 155
[2] 2 Timothy 2:15
[3] Colossians 1:28, Galatians 4:19
[4] John 8:32
[5] 1 Timothy 3:2-7
[6] James 3:1
[7] Mark 1:21-22
[8] Ephesians 4:14
[9] 2 Timothy 2:2
[10] Edited by Matthew D. Green, *Understanding the Fivefold Ministry,* "Itching Ears," R.T. Kendall, (Florida: Charisma House, 2005), p.155
[11] Ephesians 4:11-16

Chapter 11

[1] *Apostles and the Emerging Apostolic Movement*, David Cannistraci, (Ventura, CA: Regal Books, 1996).
[2] *Apostles and Prophets: The Foundation of the Church*, Peter Wagner, (Ventura, CA: Gospel Light Publications, 1999).

Chapter 12

[1] Acts 6:3-5
[2] Acts 4:13
[3] Colossians 1:22
[4] Philippians 2:13
[5] George Barna, editor, *Leaders on Leadership*, Gene Getz, "Becoming Spiritually Mature Leader," (Ventura, California: Regal, 1997), p. 90.
[6] Titus 1:9
[7] Ephesians 5:18
[8] Proverbs 23:20-21
[9] 1 Peter 5:3
[10] Philippians 2:3
[11] James 1:19
[12] 1 Timothy 5:17
[13] 1 Peter 2:12
[14] Titus 2:8
[15] Psalm 42:1
[16] Matthew 25:21
[17] Matthew 22:14 (NKJV)
[18] Matthew 20:25-28
[19] Galatians 5:16-18
[20] 2 Timothy 1:9
[21] Galatians 1:1
[22] Hebrews 12:1-2
[23] 1 Corinthians 9:24

Chapter 13

[1] Romans 12:3
[2] Larry Kreider, *Living in the Grace of God*, (Lititz, PA: House to House Publications, 2005), p. 32.
[3] John 6:38
[4] Matthew 23:11
[5] Luke 17:7-10
[6] John 15:8

Chapter 14

[1] Deuteronomy 25:4
[2] 1 Corinthians 9:9-14
[3] For more on house churches, read Larry Kreider's book, *House Church Networks: A Church for a New Generation,* available at www.dcfi.org/house2house
[4] Luke 14:28-30

Chapter 15

[1] Acts 13-14
[2] C. Peter Wagner, *Strategies for Growth* (Glendale: Regal, 1987), p. 168.
[3] 1 Timothy 1:18

About the Author

Ron Myer has more than two decades of experience in small group-based church planting, including planting and pastoring a church in Lebanon, Pennsylvania and serving on the International Apostolic Council of DOVE International. Ron serves as the Assistant International Director, dedicating his energies to leaders throughout the nation and the world. Ron also leads the DOVE USA Apostolic Team that gives oversight to the churches in the USA region.

As a fivefold apostolic minister and strong exhorter, Ron travels nationally and internationally teaching and exhorting others to rise up to their full potential as people of God. Ron's heart's cry is to see the church become the powerhouse that God designed —with the saints doing the work of ministry as they are released through home groups to set the captives free. Ron firmly believes, "the Lord is calling forth church planters to establish churches that are effective and successful."

Ron is the author of *Fivefold Ministry Made Practical* and co-author of *The Biblical Role of Elders for Today's Church*.

Ron and Bonnie have been married forty years and are still best friends. They have six children and eleven grandchildren and reside in Myerstown, Pennsylvania. Ron loves juicy hamburgers, loud pipes on his motorcycle and rides in the mountains. Bonnie enjoys being a grandma and leading a small group. "Let's make a memory" and "life should not be boring" are two of the couple's mottos for their life together.

Visit Ron's blog at www.doveusa.org/blog

**For more resources, seminar details and to order
visit www.dcfi.org   call 1.800.848.5892**

44068717R00117

Made in the USA
San Bernardino, CA
17 July 2019